CONCILIUM

THEOLOGY IN THE AGE OF RENEWAL

CONCILIUM

CONCILIUM/VOL. 24

ECUMENICAL THEOLOGY

THE
SACRAMENTS

AN
ECUMENICAL
DILEMMA

VOLUME 24

CONCILIUM
theology in the age of renewal

PAULIST PRESS
NEW YORK, N.Y. / GLEN ROCK, N.J.

PAULIST PRESS
EXECUTIVE OFFICES: 304 W. 58th Street, New York, N.Y. and 21 Harristown Road, Glen Rock, N.J.
Executive Publisher: John A. Carr, C.S.P.
Executive Manager: Alvin A. Illig, C.S.P.
Asst. Executive Manager: Thomas E. Comber, C.S.P.

EDITORIAL OFFICES: 304 W. 58th Street, New York, N.Y.
Editor: Kevin A. Lynch, C.S.P.
Managing Editor: Urban P. Intondi

Printed and bound in the United States of America by The Colonial Press Inc., Clinton, Mass.

CONTENTS

PART II

BIBLIOGRAPHICAL SURVEY

PART III

DO-C DOCUMENTATION CONCILIUM
Office of the Executive Secretary
Nijmegen, Netherlands

Preface

Hans Küng/*Tübingen, W. Germany*

Are we afraid of questions? No doubt we will be if our faith is based on some permanently fixed and closed system instead of God's revelation. Move one little stone and the whole building, the whole world of one's faith, seems to collapse. Would it not be better to test the strength of the building in time and keep a sharp eye on the weak spots?

One cannot think of the Church's life without the sacraments. The Church was never without these sacraments. Even the Reformers admitted that the sacraments have their place in the Church and in the life of the individual faithful. And yet, the teaching on the sacraments was among the most fiercely debated issues both before and after the Reformation. We have to face the fact that the sacraments have not yet been discussed with that open and sober understanding which has marked ecumenical discussion in so many fields—ecclesiology, soteriology, christology. Why?

We simply do not dare to come to grips with the doctrine on the sacraments as long as we are afraid of facing questions. If we did, we would notice very quickly that precisely this sector of theology is full of unsolved, or badly solved, old or new problems. And we would notice, too, that these problems do not date simply from the Reformation. Protestant theology is also deeply involved in attempting to clarify its own position with regard to

1

the sacraments, a task which the Reformers themselves left for their followers to solve. However strange it may appear to our present static view, sacramental theology is one of the most obscure sectors in the history of dogma, and it has never found a final formulation that was not arbitrary.

That is why it is so wrong to shy away from a discussion of the sacraments. Precisely because there are here still so many wide-open problems and because all the Churches are involved in a common search, we all have to return to the only sound foundation, even if it involves breaking up the present system, and that foundation is the original witness of God's revelation in Christ, the scriptures.

Here the problems begin. The notion of "sacrament" is not a biblical notion. The New Testament has no category of the means of grace under this name. Even baptism and eucharist have no term to cover both of them. On the other hand, it is a fact that the *musterion* of the New Testament has always been translated by "sacrament". And so, the whole range of the meaning of "mystery" passed over into the Latin "sacramentum".

Tertullian was the first to introduce the idea into the Church's language, but for him it still had a very wide meaning, and could even refer to the revelation of salvation as such. One can say that up to the 5th century the idea was fluid. Augustine was the first to deal with it methodically and to inaugurate a *doctrine* of the sacraments, and here we find the first precise definition.

Scholasticism (Hugh of St. Victor) at last gave it a place in the doctrine of salvation and the Church. The *number* of sacraments varied throughout antiquity. The number of seven sacraments was not fixed until the Scholastic period and occurs for the first time in Peter Lombard, and then only as a fact. Thomas Aquinas provided the *convenient* reasons for this number, and this 13th-century tradition was then fixed by Trent.

In order to develop this teaching fruitfully, we should, first of all, explain and explore the historical growth as such, and then undoubtedly we shall have to go back to the biblical evidence. But this will show us precisely that we must not start with a dubious notion of "sacraments" in general but rather with the individual "sacraments" as they clearly occur in the New Testament. This is the procedure in the present volume of *Concilium*. Only in this way can we find a solid basis for interdenominational dialogue so that we can proceed together in a common pursuit.

PART I
ARTICLES

James McClendon / *Larkspur, California*

Why Baptists Do Not Baptize Infants

Simply stated, Baptist practice is as follows: Baptists first seek to proclaim the Gospel. When (and only when) hearers, whether our own children or outsiders, respond by confessing faith in Christ as Lord and savior, they are accepted as candidates, immersed in the triune name in the presence of the congregation by the minister, and (in most churches) thereby admitted to membership in the congregation as brothers in Christ. It is clear, then, that what Baptists do *not* do is administer the rite to infants, neither their own nor those of their converts. Baptism is reserved for those who commit themselves to Christ in active faith, and who come to express that faith by entering the waters of the baptistry (the latter being the name for the pool within the church where baptism is performed). The age at which this takes place varies considerably both with individuals and with cultures. In Europe, late adolescence or young adulthood is the normal time; in the more culturally dominant Baptist churches of America, the age is younger; ages nine to eleven are considered normal.

I

THE NEW TESTAMENT PATTERN

If we ask the reasons for this practice, several may be offered, but the primary reasons advanced by most Baptists will be based upon scripture. There is, first of all, *the example of the New Testament apostles and Churches.* Baptists, like their medieval predecessors, the Anabaptists, have generally taken a view of Christian history which regards the New Testament era (ca. 30-100 A.D.) as a period of spiritual purity, a golden age in the Church, which was followed by a time of corruption lasting for centuries.[1]

Such a course of history is not inherently impossible—the white light of revelation *might* have shone in the 1st century in Christ and his apostles with such intensity as to purify the Church of that century in a special way. And evidence *can* be found of radical differences between the New Testament writings and the productions of the 2nd and subsequent centuries. Whether or not we regard the New Testament age as a golden age of purity, however (and the present writer, though a Baptist, does not do so), the fact remains that the Christian baptisms which the New Testament records were without exception conferred on those who came to baptism confessing their own faith-commitment. That this is so has been acknowledged by a wide variety of Christian scholars,[2] but it may be seen as well by the intelligent amateur who will give attention to the biblical material.

As preliminary, it might be noted that the great antecedent of Christian baptism, that of John the Baptist, involved, according to scripture, the conscious and responsible submission of the candidate. John called men to repentance (*metanoia:* Mk. 1, 4 and parallels), that is, to *conversion,* to a new heart evidenced by a new life. Where there was doubt about the genuineness of change, the candidates were to "bear fruits that befit repentance" (Lk. 3, 8), i.e., to show practical evidence of a new life being lived. Of course infants could not have met such conditions, and there is no evidence that John baptized any infant.[3]

[1] An example, by a well-known historian, is A. Newman, *History of Antipedobaptism* (Philadelphia, 1897).

[2] For the bibliography to 1960, see G. Beasley-Murray, *Baptism in the New Testament* (London, 1962). I am indebted to this work throughout the present article. Cf. review by R. Schnackenburg, *Bibl. Zeitschr.* 7 (1963), pp. 305-8.

[3] Two other antecedents have been proposed: proselyte baptism and that

The same considerations apply when we come to the first re-corded Christian baptisms in the Acts of the Apostles. On the day of Pentecost (Acts 2) we have the apostles, empowered by a great outpouring of the Holy Spirit, proclaiming the Good News of Christ. When it is asked what men must therefore do, Simon Peter replies "Repent" (*metanoeo:* be converted, change your attitude), and then adds: "and be baptized" (v. 38). Then "those who received his word were baptized" (v. 41). "Received" here means not merely "heard" but "embraced". It means the conscious and deliberate acceptance of the Gospel and of the Christ whom that Gospel is about. Acts would have us believe that the grace of God, and nothing less, was at work on the day of Pentecost, but it would have us see as well that the means of that grace was the proclaiming of the Gospel, leading to the re-sponse of repentance in the hearers, who then came to baptism. Acts thus proceeds to record instance after instance in this apos-tolic pattern: the Gospel is proclaimed; men hear it and respond; baptism marks their entry into a new life. So it is with Paul (Acts 9), with converts at Samaria (Acts 8) and Caesarea (Acts 10) and Philippi (Acts 16)—indeed, wherever in the New Testa-ment baptism is reported, it is the baptism of conscious and re-sponsive believers. Such examples serve to create a strong pre-sumption that only when men come to have a conscious and personal faith of their own is the Church to baptize them.

Against this line of argument two particular objections have been made. The first is that the omission by New Testament writers of the baptism of infants was an accident. They *were* baptized then, as admittedly infants were 100 years later; silence is no denial of this probable fact. This is, to be sure, an "argu-ment from silence", but, say the advocates of New Testament infant baptism, likewise the claim that the children of believers must have been baptized later is an "argument from silence"— there is no New Testament account of the baptism of a second

---

of Qumran. Of these, the former did and the latter did not accept infants. But it is noteworthy that the gospels name as antecedent not proselyte practice, nor Qumran's, but John's. Was it felt that it was similar as the others were not?

generation Christian at *any* time! [4] To this the Baptist must give assent, but add that if the "arguments from silence" thus cancel one another, then he must go on the *available* evidence, which uniformly links baptism and conscious personal commitment.

The other particular objection is that there is implicit evidence for New Testament baptism of infants in the report of the baptism of entire households, as in Acts 16. Not only is it probable that such households included infants, but Stauffer and Jeremias have argued that the word "household" in biblical use (*oikos*) has *special* reference to infants.[5] If both these points be granted, however, we are brought no further along in the argument, for many things in the New Testament are asserted of *households* of which infants as such are not capable. Thus it is not only said of the jailer that he was baptized with "all of his" (Acts 16, 33); it is also said that he *"rejoiced with all his household that he had believed in God"* (Acts 16, 34). Infants rejoicing at their father's conversion? And Acts 11, 44, by this principle, tells us (together with Acts 10) that the infants of Cornelius' household were God-fearers, heard the apostolic word, received the Spirit, *spoke with tongues* and were baptized! An age of wonders, indeed! "But surely," someone will say, "the text applies such actions to infants *only to the extent that they were capable of application.*" Exactly. And that is just the point Baptists make about the alleged inclusion of infants in the baptism of New Testament households: given the rite of New Testament baptism, is it one for which infants were conceivable candidates?

[4] O. Cullmann, *Baptism in the New Testament* (London, 1950), p. 26. (Translation of *Die Tauflehre des Neuen Testaments,* Zürich, 1948).

[5] J. Jeremias, *Infant Baptism in the First Four Centuries* (London, 1960), pp. 19ff. See replies by K. Aland, *Did the Early Church Baptize Infants?* (Philadelphia, 1963) and J. Jeremias, *The Origins of Infant Baptism* (London, 1963), all translating German works.

II

A QUESTION OF BIBLICAL THEOLOGY

The question, then, becomes finally not one of the practice of the New Testament Churches, interesting though that practice, as a clue, may be. For there could have been practices in that day, as in our own, not appropriate to the Gospel of Christ. Rather, it is a question of the *kind* of baptism the scriptures enjoin, the *doctrine* of baptism they reflect, which is at issue. If scriptural baptism could very well be applied to infants, then it was inevitable that it should be, and how soon that happened is not of first importance. If, however, it could not legitimately be so applied, then to baptize infants was to risk losing the apostolic understanding of baptism through that very misapplication. What, then, was the New Testament theology of baptism?

To speak of this briefly is of necessity to speak of New Testament theology, or rather of biblical theology as a whole. The bible finds its center in what God has done for man in time. This is true whether we read the Old Testament or the New. Each witnesses to a God who saw that it was not good for man to be alone, and who gave man not merely wife and neighbor, but himself. God coming to man in the garden in the cool of the day is the story of Genesis 3. God coming to man in Jesus of Nazareth —this is the story of the gospels. The biblical story is haunted by human perversity—idolatry and racial pride and religious self-help schemes—in reaction to God's coming, but the divine remedy for these perversions is always and only himself, in direct living encounter with his servants, drawing them to himself and to one another. The key to the gospels, then, is in the discovery that in coming to Christ, men come into God's kingdom. Christ is the king of the kingdom (Mt. 25); eternal life is to know him (Jn. 17, 3).

These lines point the way to the modest rites which accompany his ministry. During the days of his flesh, Christ is baptized, identifying himself with sinners. As the kingdom grows from the seed of his cross and resurrection and flowers on the day of Pentecost, we find the disciples summoning their hearers to baptism. Early Christian baptism retained the elements of John's baptism. (1) It was conversion-baptism (*metanoeō:* Mk. 1, 4 and parallels, e.g., Acts 2, 38). (2) It was forgiveness-baptism; the recipients confessed and were forgiven their sins (Mk. 1, 4; Acts 2, 38). (3) It admitted to the eschatological community, the "Church" (Acts 2, 41-47). But there were new notes as well. (4) It was *baptism in Jesus' name* (Acts 2, 38; 8, 16; 10, 48; 19, 5), or, later, the triune name (Mt. 28, 19f.). The expression "in the name of" in biblical use may mean "on the authority of", or it may mean "establishing a relationship to". The context of its use here justifies both senses: baptism was by divine authority; it established a relationship to Christ as Lord. (5) It was, then, *confession-baptism*—the sign of commitment of the baptized. In it he "called upon the name of the Lord" for salvation (cf. Acts 22, 16). (6) It was *baptism in the Holy Spirit* (Mk. 1, 8 and parallels, e.g., Acts 1, 5; 2, 38; 8, 12-17; 9, 17-19, etc.). The sharp separation between receiving the Spirit and the "mere external rite" of baptism found in later writers is not present here. There are, of course, other emphases, but these at least were characteristic.[6]

As the first Christians practiced baptism, their interpretation of it was deepened and clarified, notably by the apostle Paul. Paul's chief contribution was to link baptism more vividly with the death and resurrection of Christ. To do this he seized upon the imagery of burial and raising involved in total immersion (evidently the regular New Testament mode, as the verb, *baptizein*, to dip, suggests: Rom. 6, 1ff.). Baptism, said Paul, means that Christ's death was our own, that his resurrection was our own. Thus he emphasized baptism as union with Christ, demanding *ethical* behavior of the newly-crucified-with-Christ believer. Again he seized the image of *washing* (1 Cor. 6, 11) to make the same ethical emphasis. For Paul, religion (union with Christ) and responsible behavior converge—in baptism! Particularly does

---

[6] With this summary compare W. Flemington, *The New Testament Doctrine of Baptism* (London, 1948).

he warn that neither the Lord's supper nor baptism can be treated as an automatic prophylactic against sin (1 Cor. 10, 1ff.). For him, baptism is the means of entry into the one "body"—his term for union both with Christ and with the brethren (cf. 1 Cor. 12, 13; Gal. 3, 26f.; Eph. 4, 4-6). Paul's teaching may be compared with that of John (Jn. 3), who links baptism (v. 5) with the Spirit, the new birth (v. 3) and faith (v. 16)—these belong together in the apostolic scheme of things.

Space forbids a wider survey. It seems that we have enough to show that Jesus, at the summit of the biblical revelation, acted to bring God's presence to men in such a way as to maintain the divine freedom and initiative as well as human responsiveness. He did this by giving himself to men in direct and personal encounter—an encounter in which men were made whole and joined to one another, marked by a baptism that was at once God's Word to man and man's answering word to God.

III

A PEDOBAPTIST VIEW

With the above summary may be compared the work of the Swiss Reformed theologian, O. Cullmann, who also grants that New Testament theology, rather than New Testament practice alone, must be determinative for us. Since Cullmann reaches a different conclusion, it may be well to note the crucial points of difference in his account. His strongest emphasis is upon the primacy of God's grace in baptism, best reflected, he believes, in the practice of infant baptism. Just as Christ died for all before any responded in faith, so baptism sets one in the body of Christ before he can respond.[7] To this our answer would be to agree upon the primacy of grace in baptism, but to urge that that grace is not obscured but rather glorified by the response of a lively, conscious candidate, acknowledging that grace has come to *him*. How surprised the apostle Paul would be to hear that his con-

[7] O. Cullmann, *op. cit.*, Chs. 2 and 3.

version-baptism was of a sort which obscured the primacy of grace!

Cullmann also adduces Jewish circumcision. Just as it was a rite of initiation which for infants preceded faith, so by analogy can baptism precede faith, whether or not it did so in the New Testament examples.[8] But, we reply, the analogy between these two *is* an analogy. And in an analogy we expect to find points both of similarity *and of difference*. Whether we have, with respect to the necessity for accompanying faith, a similarity or a difference in circumcision and in baptism is just what is at issue. The one passage which is generally put forward as establishing the identity of the two (Col. 2, 11f.) directly compares circumcision not with baptism but with Christ's death (the "stripping off" of *all* his flesh—total circumcision!). Then baptism is said to relate *us* to that death. The two rites remain analogues only, for the point of similarity in question is not established in this text.

Other proposed New Testament arguments for infant baptism similarly fall short. The blessing of children (Mt. 19, 13ff. and parallels) may justify the blessing of infants by the Church; it surely encourages us to bring children to Christ. What it docs *not* do is to encourage baptism prior to faith. (If it be asked what is then the state of the unbaptized infant, of whatever parentage, dying in infancy, we must answer that his state in death is as his state in life—in both cases he is in the care of God, who is love, 1 Jn. 4, 8.) Signs, including the awesome sign that is baptism, are for those able to receive them, and baptism, like the crucified and risen Christ whom it signifies, is received by grace *through faith* (cf. Eph. 2, 8).

IV

A Baptist Confession

In summary, then, Baptists reject infant baptism because it seems to us contrary to the practice of the New Testament

[8] *Ibid.*, ch. 4.

Church, and because it fails to reflect either the theology of New Testament *baptism* or the way in which Christ's *salvation* comes to man in personal encounter. Baptists are accused by their brethren of "rebaptizing" those who come to them from pedo-baptist Churches. We do not intend to do so. Rather, we regard infant "baptism" as another rite than that of the New Testament, and we understand ourselves to be *baptizing* such candidates for the first time.

At the same time, we acknowledge the reality of Christian faith and life in others, and we rejoice in it. That the practice of infant baptism has much to commend it cannot be denied. It has met genuine needs in the Church and has coexisted with authentic Christian character as truly as has believer's baptism. And we Baptists acknowledge that *our* understanding of baptism might be mistaken or inadequate.[9]

We inquire of our brethren, however, whether they may not also reconsider their own practice in this matter. Has not the persistence of believer's baptism through church history been for a purpose? [10] Does not the existence of millions of "baptized" pagans in Europe and America challenge the usual practice? Can anyone in a post-Constantinian age justify the continuance of a rite weighted with Constantinian presuppositions? Is it not the role of the Church again to *be* the Church, and the role of her baptism to identify her sons? [11] Such questions Baptists lovingly put to their sister Churches.

[9] Cf. G. Beasley-Murray, *Baptism Today and Tomorrow* (London, 1966), ch. 4.

[10] For the history of baptism, see A. Gilmore, ed., *Christian Baptism: A Fresh Attempt to Understand the Rite in Terms of Scripture, History, and Theology* (London, 1959).

[11] This is the plea of K. Barth in *The Teaching of the Church regarding Baptism* (London, 1948), a translation of *Die Kirchliche Lehre von der Taufe* (Theologische Studien 14, Zollikon-Zürich).

Michael Hurley, S.J./*Dublin, Ireland*

What Can Catholics Learn from the Infant Baptism Controversy?

The traditional practice of infant baptism in post-war years has been a subject of considerable controversy in continental (European) Protestantism, in the Church of England (Anglican) and in the Baptist Churches. The controversy in each case has had its own particular origins and scope; nevertheless, it may be seen as part of a whole movement of ecclesial self-criticism and renewal, centered very understandably and appropriately on the Church's rite of initiation.

I

THE BAPTIST CHURCHES

In the Baptist Churches the practical questions are: Should we continue to rebaptize all those who become Baptists? Is infant baptism no baptism? What should our infant dedication rite mean and do? In their approach to these questions, leading Baptist scholars in Britain are endeavoring to modify the traditional anabaptist viewpoint and practice. The occasion and immediate origin of this movement would seem to be ecumenical. It appears to derive from the involvement of the Baptist Union in the British Council of Churches.

Paradoxically, while non-Baptist churchmen and theologians

16

now tend to depreciate or reject infant baptism, Baptists are beginning to consider it more sympathetically and appreciatively. The following quotation clearly indicates the new trend:

> The rebaptism as believers of those who have received baptism in infancy constitutes a blow at the heart of the Christian faith. As there is one Lord and one faith, so there is but one baptism. . . . Baptism stands under the *ephapax* of redemption. The whole meaning of the rite hinges on its once-for-allness, its unrepeatability. The assertion of the partial nature of infant baptism and the serious theological distortion it involves does not carry with it the unqualified dismissal of it as "no baptism"; rather does the eschatological nature of the rite forbid so negative a verdict. For no baptism can lack its proleptic element, and every baptism points forward for its completion and fulfillment.[1]

This is highly controversial writing for a Baptist, but the author is no mere voice crying in the wilderness. The new trend of thought was heard on June 3, 1965, at the Eleventh Congress of the World Baptist Alliance at Miami Beach. Here Dr. Beasley-Murray (the English translator of Professor Schnackenburg's *Das Heilsgeschehen bei der Taufe nach dem Apostel Paulus*) affirmed that sprinkling should be recognized as a proper mode of administering the sacrament because burial (symbolized by immersion) was only one element of the baptismal symbolism and because the *Didache* sanctioned this mode. He also affirmed that those baptized in infancy who have been "duly admitted into membership of a Church on profession of faith" should not be rebaptized on becoming Baptists. Only those "without any subsequent profession of faith or Church membership" should receive believers' baptism. In addition, Dr. Beasley-Murray indicated his approval of "a rite of initiation into the Christian society" for infants. Such rites are becoming increasingly common among Baptists. They are considered as initiating the child

[1] N. Clark, "The Theology of Baptism," in *Christian Baptism*, ed. A. Gilmore (London, 1959), p. 325.

"within the sphere of the Church", "into its midst", "its outer circle". "Initiation into Christ and his body in the full sense" is considered as given only by believers' baptism.[2]

What can the Roman Catholic theologian learn from this controversial thinking about infant baptism among Baptists?

1. He can come to realize how unprofitable it is simply to criticize the Baptists or any other Christian communion and how his ecumenical responsibility lies rather in discreetly helping the new trends in each confession to establish themselves and to develop.

2. He can learn that dialogue with Baptists is immediately possible and could be mutually rewarding on the subject of infant dedication. Roman Catholics and Anglicans are increasingly interested in the restoration of the catechumenate and its liturgical ordering.

3. He can deepen his appreciation of the tradition that accepted infant baptism. "There is," according to Dr. Beasley-Murray, "everything to be said in favor of the Church's providing for children a solemn rite of entry into its midst. . . . Baptists are aware that there are needs that infant baptism seeks to meet and that ought to be met by some means or other." [3]

4. In view of the fact that the strongest argument advanced against infant baptism is pastoral rather than academic, he can learn that the most convincing argument in favor of infant baptism will be evidence that in practice it works.

[2] G. R. Beasley-Murray, "Baptists and the Baptism of Other Churches," in *The Truth that Makes Men Free*. Official Report of the Eleventh Congress of the World Baptist Alliance (Nashville, 1966), pp. 261-73. This paper is reproduced with some modifications by the author in his latest book, *Baptism Today and Tomorrow* (London, 1966), pp. 145-72. Cf. also A. Gilmore, *Baptism and Christian Unity* (London, 1966).

[3] A. Gilmore, *op. cit.*, pp. 136, 162.

II

THE CHURCH OF ENGLAND

According to Dr. Beasley-Murray, "the most striking change of attitude to the New Testament teaching on baptism . . . is manifest in the Anglican communion." [4] The controversy on infant baptism has indeed reached such proportions in the Church of England that, in the opinion of the same writer, "it is possible that this Church will be in the van of baptismal reform within the Church of Christ in Europe, with unforeseeable consequences for the Church in the rest of the world".[5] In regard to the Church of England, the occasion and immediate origins of the controversy are pastoral and domestic rather than ecumenical. The immediate issue is not so much (as in the case of the Baptists) how to improve relations with other Churches as how to improve the religious life of Anglicans and how to bridge the gap between nominal and effective membership of the Church of England.

Two facts dominate the controversy:

1. A high percentage of baptized infants no longer grow up to be practicing Christians. Out of every hundred children born in England, 67 are said to be baptized by Anglicans, but of these only nine "remain faithful to the extent of making their communion once a year at Easter".[6]

2. Despite this fact, the demand for baptism has not been affected. It continues even from those who have only a minimal, if any, connection with the Church.

These two facts have caused the Church of England to devote considerable work and study to almost every aspect of Christian initiation, and they have given rise, in particular, to the vexed question of "indiscriminate baptism", i.e., whether or not discriminatory tests or restrictive disciplines should be applied, whether or not the font as well as the table should be fenced.[7]

---

[4] "The Baptismal Controversy in the British Scene," in K. Aland, *Did the Early Church Baptize Infants?* (London, 1963), p. 20.

[5] A. Gilmore, *op. cit.,* p. 169.

[6] *Baptism To-Day* (London, 1949), p. 8.

[7] The following reports of the Joint Committees on Baptism, Con-

To this question[8] some Anglicans say "no". Every opportunity, they agree, should be taken to declare both what baptism means and what it demands, but no one who asks should ultimately be refused because "one of the things infant baptism testifies to is the priority of God's grace over our faith, the priority of Christ's work over our response". Other Anglicans go to the opposite extreme in their answer; they advocate the abolition of infant baptism and the institution of a new rite of naming and blessing and admission to the catechumenate, which would be administered to all infants. Baptism would be deferred and, as in scripture, associated with personal commitment and faith. The whole process of Christian initiation would be reintegrated in a single, unified and, perhaps on occasion, continuous act. A third group would reserve the new rite exclusively for those who do not satisfy the minimal requirements. They would permit infant baptism where "the child is likely to be brought up in the context of active faith and discipleship", where there is some assurance of his Christian upbringing, but they would consider adult believers' baptism as the normal practice.

After a quarter of a century of debate, the Church of England remains deeply divided on this issue and as yet no official directive has been issued. At a conference in 1965 sponsored by the Parish and People Movement, the Anglicans in a special commission voted decisively against the first answer, and, with a very slight majority, in favor of the second as opposed to the third, i.e., in favor of the abolition of infant baptism. The conference as a whole, however, after an extremely tense debate, refused to vote on the matter.[9]

---

firmation and Holy Communion of the Convocations of Canterbury and York are particularly noteworthy: *Confirmation To-Day* (London, 1944); *The Theology of Christian Initiation* (London, 1948); *Baptism To-Day* (London, 1949); *Baptism and Confirmation To-Day* (London, 1955). Cf. also *Baptism and Confirmation*, a report submitted by the Church of England Liturgical Commission (London, 1959); *Crisis for Baptism*, ed. B. Moss (London, 1965).

[8] *Baptism To-Day*, pp. 24-31; *Crisis for Baptism*, pp. 22-39. Similar views were put forward in France before the hierarchy issued its directives. Cf. *Semaine religieuse de Paris*, February 26, 1966, pp. 241-51.

[9] *Crisis for Baptism*, pp. 25, 28. There were 23 Anglican votes for the

What can the Roman Catholic theologian learn from this infant baptism controversy in the Church of England?

1. He can learn to give closer consideration to the view that "in the New Testament adult baptism is the norm, and it is only in the light of this fact that the doctrine and practice of baptism can be understood".[10] He can thus learn to be more cautious in applying a theology of adult baptism to infant baptism.

2. He can learn how urgent it is to restudy the doctrine and to reconsider the theology of original sin. He may feel less embarrassed in this matter than Anglicans who state that "our Thirty-Nine Articles admittedly seem nearer to the more extreme positions of Augustine and Calvin than to the more moderate positions of Trent",[11] but can he agree that "infant baptism is not to be defended by any argument asserting that the child is thereby saved from being penalized eternally"? [12] If so, how is the necessity and meaning of infant baptism to be understood?

3. He can learn from the Church of England's emphasis on Christian initiation as a whole and its maintenance of the traditional sequence (baptism, confirmation, communion) a much-needed awareness of the anomalous character of present Roman liturgical practice and of its embarrassing effects on our theologizing about confirmation and worship. If confirmation preceded communion (as it should) the *Constitution on the Sacred Liturgy* might not have failed to emphasize the essential missionary aspect of Christian worship.

---

abolition of infant baptism and 21 for its retention in the case of the children of committed Christians. In the commission as a whole, 26 voted in favor of the latter proposal, 23 in favor of the former.

[10] *Baptism and Confirmation*, p. x.

[11] *Baptism To-Day*, p. 45.

[12] *Unity Begins at Home* (London, 1964), p. 65.

III

CONTINENTAL PROTESTANTISM

The controversy on infant baptism in continental (European) Protestantism is mainly associated with the names of Karl Barth, Oscar Cullmann, Joachim Jeremias and Kurt Aland.[13] It differs from the Baptist and Anglican controversies insofar as its immediate origins are more academic and historical than ecumenical and pastoral. Indeed, the controversy is not at present about infant baptism in itself, whether it should be abandoned or retained, but about its origins, whether or not it was practiced in the first two centuries, and therefore about its theological justification, whether and to what extent there is any evidence for it in the New Testament and the early Church. Despite their differences Jeremias and Aland both agree that infant baptism should be retained.

It would seem that this infant baptism controversy has played a part in helping the non-Roman Churches to reach the more positive attitude to tradition, evidenced, for example, in the report on "Scripture, Tradition and Traditions" of the Fourth World Conference on Faith and Order (Montreal, 1963).[14] Whether or not this is so, the first thing the Roman Catholic theologian can learn from the controversy is a new appreciation of the truth that bible and Church, scripture and tradition, however their relationship be explained, may in no way be divorced or opposed. He can also learn to admit that the connection in time and thought between the practice of infant baptism and the doctrine of original sin is as yet by no means clear and needs still further study.

In his classical work, *The Ideas of the Fall and of Original*

[13] K. Barth, *The Teaching of the Church regarding Baptism* (London, 1948); O. Cullmann, *Baptism in the New Testament* (London, 1950); J. Jeremias, *Infant Baptism in the First Four Centuries* (London, 1960); K. Aland, *Did the Early Church Baptize Infants?* (London, 1963); J. Jeremias, *The Origins of Infant Baptism* (London, 1963).

[14] *The Fourth World Conference on Faith and Order*. The Report from Montreal (1963), edited by P. C. Rodger and L. Vischer (London, 1964), pp. 50-60.

Sin, the Anglican theologian N. P. Williams maintained that the practice preceded the doctrine in time.[15] Aland, however, holds the opposite view and explains the emergence of infant baptism as a result of the emergence of the idea of original sin. He adduces evidence "to demonstrate that the belief in the sinlessness of infants was held continuously until the time of Tertullian".[16] Jeremias controverts this evidence, but his basic criticism is that Aland, in emphasizing baptism as a bath of cleansing, "projects back into the apostolic period the shriveled understanding of baptism which made its appearance in many places, though by no means everywhere, in the 2nd century . . . and [which] saw in it to an increasing extent only the sacrament of the great remission of sins".[17]

This brings us to the final lesson that the Roman Catholic theologian can learn from the whole infant baptism controversy: infant baptism is still a practice in search of a theology. As Jeremias has shown, the New Testament may provide some slight evidence for the practice, but it provides no exposition of its meaning. Like the article in the Nicene Creed, the New Testament theology of baptism seems to refer to adult baptism. In that case, however, it is not enough to insist that the negative and positive aspects of baptism are complementary and mutually explanatory because the negative effect of adult baptism is the remission of sins—of actual rather than original sin—and this effect is not applicable to infants. On the other hand, the New Testament theology of redemption would seem to imply that all mankind needs to be liberated, that every man coming into this world, and not just every adult sinner, is in need of salvation, in need of Christ, and that if he does not find this salvation, he is lost in this life and in the next. The neglect of soteriology in Roman Catholic systematic theology may well be a significant factor in the present unsatisfactory state of our understanding of original sin and of infant baptism.

[15] London, 1927, p. 223.
[16] *Op. cit.,* pp. 103-6.
[17] *The Origins of Infant Baptism,* pp. 77-85.

Max Thurian/*Taizé, France*

Confession in the Evangelical Churches

There is a certain lack of continuity in the Protestant attitude toward confession. This makes it difficult to ascertain the exact position of the Evangelical, Lutheran or Reformed Churches. Roughly speaking, we can distinguish three phases: (1) the thought of the Reformers, Luther and Calvin; (2) the anti-Catholic reaction against confession; (3) the revival of the practice of confession as part of the "cure of souls" and "spiritual retreats", in the atmosphere of ecumenical goodwill.

We shall try to summarize these three phases schematically, within the confines of an article that has little space for intricacies.

I

THE REFORMERS

Luther maintains the sacramental value of absolution. In the *Babylonian Captivity of the Church of God*,[1] he explicitly states that he accepts three sacraments: baptism, penance and bread. He is a little hesitant, however, because of the lack of a divinely instituted sign, and so penance becomes a renewal of baptism.[2]

---

[1] *Luthers Werke* VI (Weimar), p. 501.
[2] *Ibid.*, p. 572.

Melancthon keeps absolution as the third sacrament: "If the rites ordained by God with the promise of grace are to be called sacraments . . . the sacraments are baptism, the Lord's supper and absolution, which is the sacrament of repentance." [3] The Confession of Augsburg declares: "Strictly speaking, penance consists of these two parts: (1) contrition, or the terrors of the conscience which knows it has sinned; (2) faith through the Gospel, or absolution; and he [the sinner] believes that his sins are forgiven for Christ's sake, comforts his conscience and sets it free from its terrors." [4] Luther does not hold that confession is absolutely obligatory, but he allows that the faithful should be strongly recommended in church to confess regularly.

In 1529 he added to the second edition of his Long Catechism a "short exhortation on confession".[5] He begins by saying: "We have always taught that confession should be a matter for free choice." [6] He highly recommends the practice of private confession, "our dear confession", as he calls it. "If a poor beggar heard that in a certain place lavish alms, money or clothes were being distributed, would it be necessary for a policeman to take him there? If you are poor and miserable, go to confession and make use of this saving medicine. . . . If, on the other hand, you despise this treasure and are too proud to confess your sins, we infer that you are not a Christian at all and should not share in the sacrament [of the Lord's supper]. You despise what no Christian should despise, which means that you cannot get forgiveness for your sins and that you despise the Gospel." Luther does not want to allow "the enjoyment of our freedom" to those who, under the pretext of being evangelical, dispense themselves from every discipline and from confession in particular. It is better to be "compelled" to go to confession, to fast, etc., "than to despise the free and joyful discipline of going to confession, fasting, etc. As the thirsty deer craves for running water, my soul thirsts for the Word of the Lord, absolution and the sacrament".[7]

[3] *Apologia confessionis,* Art. 13 (7).
[4] Art. 12, "De paenitentia".
[5] *Les livres symboliques* (Paris, 1947), pp. 227-33.
[6] *Ibid.,* p. 227.
[7] *Ibid.,* p. 233.

Calvin rejects the sacrament of penance, but he keeps private, non-obligatory confession. It is worth noting that his criticism of the sacrament of penance dates almost entirely from his first version of the *Institutes* (1536). The 1539 and 1541 editions contain important modifications to his criticism. Calvin's thought develops considerably, doubtless as a result of the influence of Strasbourg and his exercise of the ministry. Into the 1539 passage where he says that pastors are "ordained by God to instruct us how we can overcome sin and to assure us of God's goodness for our consolation", he inserted from 1545 onward this important development: "For although the office of mutual admonition is common to all Christians, it is especially enjoined upon ministers. For just as we are to comfort each other each in his due place, so we see that ministers are ordained by God as witnesses and almost as pledges to give to consciences the assurance of the forgiveness of their sins, so that it is said that they forgive sins and unbind souls (Mt. 16, 19; 18, 18; Jn. 20, 23). When we see that this is accorded to them, let us think that it is for our profit." [8]

Pastors are not only witnesses announcing the forgiveness of sins; their function is not only to preach the Gospel; they are, as it were, guarantors of this forgiveness. For this is what is meant by "pledge". Thus, pastors are to answer to the troubled conscience for God's promises in Jesus Christ; they are a kind of security or guarantee when they unbind souls through the Good News of the Gospel in absolution. They are guarantors of the mercy of God so much so that "it is said that they forgive sins and unbind souls". There can be no doubt that Calvin is here interpreting the words of Jesus to the apostles after his resurrection (Jn. 20, 23) and the power of the keys (Mt. 16, 19; 18, 18) in the traditional sense of the sacrament of absolution: the Church, by the word of her ministers in the promise of Jesus Christ, has the power to forgive sins and unbind souls.

Of course we must not exaggerate Calvin's thought and we

---

[8] *Institution chretienne* (1560), Bk. II, Ch. 4, para. 12.

must hasten to add that the whole context of his reflections upon penance and the power of the keys makes it clear that he attributes this power of absolution not to the Church or to the minister as such, but insofar as they announce the Gospel. Has authentic Christian tradition ever thought otherwise? Has it ever divided the ministry of Christ and his minister except in theologically barren periods?

II

THE ANTI-CATHOLIC REACTION

This is a reaction in the name of freedom of confession and under the influence of a non-sacerdotal conception of the ministry. The Reformers had asserted this Christian freedom, but they were nevertheless convinced of the usefulness of a discipline freely undertaken. Later there was so much emphasis on freedom that discipline suffered. The emphasis on the transcendence and freedom of God made it less easy to think of an efficacious sign than of a word requiring only the free acceptance of the believer. The idea of a sacramental sign effecting what it signifies became almost scandalous and readily dismissed as witchcraft. This attitude is like the scandal of the scribes when Christ forgave the sins of the paralytic (Mt. 9, 1-8). In fact, their theology wanted to safeguard at all costs the transcendence of God. Forgiving sins is making use of a power that belongs to God alone. How can someone who is a man like other men have the right to release his neighbor from the guilt that lies upon him? This absolution can only be something that he preaches and that the hearer must make his own through faith in order to obtain the certainty that he has been forgiven by God.

We sometimes find this notion in Protestant thought. The affirmation of the transcendence of God must exclude the possibility of the Church declaring the forgiveness of sins or of granting true absolution, but it is a Judaizing notion that has been superseded by the incarnation. The Son of man, indeed, has power on earth to forgive sins. In his manhood Christ can give absolution, and the sign that he can is his curing of the paralytic. "When the crowds saw it, they were afraid, and they glorified God who had given such authority to men" (Mt. 9, 8). The power to forgive, like the power to cure, is a privilege of the Son of man which is also given "to men" insofar as they are united to Jesus Christ in the Church. The Church, the body of Christ—that is, the manhood of Jesus working in the world today—still has this power of absolution. She does not, therefore, only preach forgiveness but really grants it. The Church has not only the duty to preach the divine mercy in order to arouse faith and the assurance of forgiveness, but she has the power really to forgive sins by the efficacious sign of absolution. This ministry of absolution is part of the mission of the apostles and the Church. Jesus compared this forgiveness to his cure of the paralytic and made the cure the sign of the forgiveness. The Church declares the absolution of sins; she miraculously sets on his feet a man crippled by his misdeeds. It is a work of resurrection; it is the risen Christ at work in her. It is the risen Christ who on Easter night gave to his apostles, and through them to the Church, the power and the mission to forgive sins. "He said to them: 'Peace be with you. As the Father has sent me, even so I send you.' And when he had said this he breathed on them and said to them, 'Receive the Holy Spirit. If you forgive the sins of any, they are forgiven; if you retain the sins of any, they are retained'" (Jn. 20, 22-23).

This reaction in the name of Christian freedom and the transcendence of God also combines with the development of individualism within the Protestant tradition. The vision of the Church as the community of forgiven sinners gives way to a spirituality of the individual alone before his God. Confession is an affair between God and the individual; the pastor only has the duty to preach the Word of divine mercy, the fruits of which each man receives by individual faith, in his personal relationship to God.

III

THE REVIVAL OF CONFESSION

We can note the influence of pietism in the Evangelical Churches; it resulted from the rediscovery of communal responsibility and the practice of the "cure of souls" accompanied by confession and even absolution. Jean-Christophe Blumhardt remarked upon this rediscovery in his ministry. "He fell upon his knees," he wrote about one of his first penitents, "and I gave him absolution by the laying on of hands. When he stood up, he was transformed, his face shining with joy and gratitude. . . . The increase in the numbers of people who come to me is so great that it takes me from seven in the morning until late at night to see them all. . . . Several times I have given absolution. I thought it right to repeat this act with hearts so broken. I have caused a large number of people to come back. . . ." [9] The awakening of his parish went with the revival of confession.

Nearer our time we can note the influence of the Oxford Group, whence arose Moral Rearmament. The militants in the Oxford Group insisted on the need for the examination of conscience, for confession (sometimes in public), and for the maintenance of a sort of freely chosen spiritual director. Many pastors and faithful rediscovered in this way the benefits of confession and of the "cure of souls". Of course, in this rediscovery the emphasis was not so much on the sacramental theology of absolution as on the "cure of souls", in which confession has a place, followed by the assurance of forgiveness in the name of the Gospel. In fact, evangelical theology is afraid to give the confessor too much importance; it dislikes the "I" of *Absolvo te;* it prefers the confessor to efface himself to some extent behind the Gospel of Christ who releases from sin.

The rediscovery of confession and absolution within Protestantism has been greatly helped by the renewal of the communal conception of the Church, particularly with the ecumenical movement. We can see this revival in German Lutheranism.

[9] See E. Grin, *Jean-Christophe Blumhardt* (Geneva, 1952).

The increasing practice of spiritual retreats also contributed to the development of the "cure of souls" with confession and absolution. In communities such as Taizé in France or Grandchamp in Switzerland, the practice of confession and absolution has become usual in the ministry to people on retreat.

This revival has had to encounter certain difficulties. The popularization of psychoanalytic doctrines and psychotherapy often makes a clear idea of sin difficult. So much has been said about guilt complexes that often the Christian no longer knows the ways in which he really is a sinner. It is true, on the other hand, that too much emphasis has often been placed on personal sin and not enough on the Christian's social responsibility. We need now to recover this social dimension of sin against humanity and to get away from an individualistically pietist view of confession.

Modern youth distrusts institutions and established forms; it craves for authenticity and inwardness. Its criticism of institutions does not favor the use of traditional sacramental forms. While preserving the objectivity of the efficacious sign of absolution and without falling into the mere sharing of moral problems, we should perhaps now try to evolve freer and more spontaneous forms of confession, in which the confessor and the penitent are in a friendly situation rather than in the solemnity of a liturgical relationship that many people find uncomfortable. And here we come to a more general problem. The Church in her service to modern men must both exercise her objective sacramental ministry and place herself at their disposal in a simple and friendly way. The word "power" must constantly give way to the word "service"; the power through the Gospel to forgive sins must become a friendly and simple service, in authentic and human forms.[10]

[10] Cf. M. Thurian, *Confession* (London, 1958).

Walter Kasper/*Tübingen, W. Germany*

Confession outside the Confessional

The sacrament of penance,[1] particularly its judicial character (*DS* 1679, 1685f.), appears to be as strong a point of controversy as ever between the separated Churches. This applies in spite of the various new ideas and approaches to the sacrament that have come from the Protestants[2] who, having discovered the weak point in their theology and practice, are now seeking to regain concepts long ago set aside. As it happens, their loss has proved something of a blessing, for it has led their theologians to discover in scripture and tradition a wealth of possible forms of the sacrament and to reintroduce these in a shape suited to the times.

Catholic theology and pastoral practice could learn a great deal from Protestant discoveries. The Catholic Church is con-

---

[1] Recent Catholic literature on the sacrament of penance: F. Charrière, "Le pouvoir d'ordre et le pouvoir de jurisdiction dans le sacrement de pénitence," in *Divus Thomas* 23 (1945), pp. 191-213; E. Doronzo, *Tractatus dogmaticus de paenitentia* I-IV (Milwaukee, 1949-53); J. Ternus, "Die sakramentale Lossprechung als richterlicher Akt," in *Zeit. f. kath. Theol.* 71 (1949), pp. 214-30; P. Galtier, *De Paenitentia* (Rome, 1950); B. Poschmann, "Die innere Struktur des Busssakramentes," in *Münch. theol. Zeit.* I (1950), pp. 1-11; P. Anciaux, *The Sacrament of Penance* (London & New York, 1962); K. Rahner, "Forgotten Truths concerning the Sacrament of Penance," in *Theological Investigations* II (London & Baltimore), pp. 135-75; F. Heggen, *Boeteviering en private biecht* (Roermond, 1964).

[2] A useful overall view is offered by L. Klein in his *Evangelisch-lutherische Beichte. Lehre u. Praxis* (Paderborn, 1961).

vinced she has preserved the essential nature of the biblical message, but in concentrating so exclusively on essentials she has lost sight of other alternatives open to her. This has led to a considerable impoverishment of Christian life and, more specifically, of Church practice. Evidence from all sides shows a crisis in the sacrament of penance rooted in a dissatisfaction with the forms we now have. Fortunately, out of this discontent a search for new forms is developing.[3]

Vatican Council II explicitly encouraged new thinking when it said in the *Constitution on the Sacred Liturgy:* "The rite and formulas for the sacrament of penance are to be revised so that they give more luminous expression to both the nature and effect of the sacrament." [4] That such a directive can be given at all presupposes that the present form of the sacrament fails to explain its nature and effect adequately, that, in a word, it does not meet the Constitution's demand. Ecumenically, it would at this stage be much more useful if we were to take the bull by the horns and join the Protestants in their search instead of perpetuating what could be an endless argument on either side about the *status quo* between the previous theology and pastoral practice.

I

THE SIN-FORGIVING POWER OF GOD'S WORD

Scripture testifies that conversion of spirit is the most fundamental demand made on mankind.[5] Scripture is not interested

[3] R. Meurice, "Les celebrations de la pénitence, suggestions et expériences," in *Maison-Dieu* 56 (1958), pp. 76-95; H. Schürmann, "Osterfeier u. Busssakrament," in *Lit. Jahrbuch,* 8 (1958), pp. 11-18; Th. Rast, *Von der Beichte zum Sakrament der Busse* (Düsseldorf, 1964); H. Meyer, "Beichte und (oder) Seelenführung" in *Orientierung* 29 (1965), pp. 133-7; J. Dreissen, "Neuorientierung der Busskatechese," in *Katechet. Blätt.* 91 (1966), pp. 217-22; *idem,* "Die liturgische Eneuerung des Busssakramentes," in Herder-Korrespondenz 13 (1958/9), pp. 297-304; *idem,* "Sinn und Möglichkeiten einer liturgischen Eneuerung des Busssakramentes," *ibid.,* 14 (1959/60), pp. 180-9; *idem,* "Äusserungen junger Katholiken über das Busssakrament," *ibid.,* 15 (1960/1), pp. 292-6.

[4] *Constitution on the Sacred Liturgy,* n. 72.

[5] On the biblical concept of "conversion", cf. E. Würthwein and

simply in repentance and reparation for each individual trans-
gression of the divine law, but in "a new attitude of man to God
and to his will for us, the spirit of this attitude impregnating
every area of human activity". Scripture encourages man to turn
full face to God so that man may be aware of him and take him
seriously in all his decisions.[6] A conversion understood in this
way is but the negative expression of what faith expresses positively: the foundation of human existence in God's grace. Faith
of this sort justifies man in God's eyes (Rom. 1, 17; 3, 22; Gal.
2, 16 et passim). Through this faith God purifies the hearts of
men (Acts 15, 9).

The problem we have to face involves, first of all, the question
of a new and personal faith that squares up to the first commandment: "I am the Lord your God." Faith such as this is not just
a necessary attitude of mind but the very spirit of Christian
sacramental penance. For this reason, until the high Middle Ages,
the main stress in the sacrament of penance was on the penitent's
personal penitential acts rather than on the absolution that the
priest mediated.[7] The first consideration in all attempts at renewal
must be how personal faith and interior conversion can most
readily be activated and deepened.

But faith is possible only through revelation (Rom. 10, 17).
The proclaimed Word of the Gospel is an effective Word—it
effects what it says. Thus it is that a sermon not only speaks of
the forgiveness of sins, reconciliation and peace with God; it
actually brings about forgiveness, reconciliation and peace. God's
Word possesses a sacramental function.[8] One sees this in the

---

J. Behm who have an article on the subject in *Theol. Wörterbuch z. N.T.*
IV, pp. 972-1004; R. Schnackenburg, *The Moral Teaching of the New
Testament* (London & New York, 1964), pp. 15-25; *idem*, "Metanoia,"
in *Lex. f. Theol. u. Kirche* VII, pp. 356-9 (Lit.).

[6] E. Würthwein, *op. cit.*, pp. 980ff.

[7] B. Poschmann, *Penance and Anointing of the Sick* (London & New
York, 1964).

[8] From the plentiful literature on this theme I would mention: F.
Arnold, *Dienst am Glauben* (Untersuchung zur Theologie der Seelsorge,
I) (Freiburg i. Br., 1948); H. Schlier, *Wort Gottes* (Würzburg, 1958);
K. Schelkle, *Jüngerschaft und Apostelamt* (Freiburg i. Br., 1957), pp.

Roman liturgy when, after reading the Gospel, the celebrant says: "Through the words of the Gospel may our sins be blotted out."

To appreciate the full span of Catholic doctrine on this subject, one should contrast this concept of the sacrament of penance with Trent's view of it as something merely in the service of the proclamation of the Word (*DS* 1670, 1709). It is the heretical absolutization of Trent's concept that is to be condemned, and no more than this. The sacrament of penance is simply a particular realization of God's Word, an effective and symbolic representation of it that is at once judgment and reprieve. Its heart and its spirit consist in the faithful hearing and following of the proclaimed Word that is God's judgment and his graciousness. Faith that accepts God's Word in this way automatically embraces the Church; such faith has within its very roots all the essential elements of the sacrament of penance.

Faith is genuine only when realized in love (Gal. 5, 6). It is this that enables scripture and all early Church tradition to designate those fruits of faith, prayer, fasting and almsgiving as the means through which sins are forgiven;[9] through them our everyday sins can be blotted out. Today a particularly appropriate form of Christian penance and an expression of sincere faith are Christian acts of love directed toward the brother. The tradition, in some countries now quite widespread, of giving money or material goods to a recognized organization represents a type of penance that excellently expresses the fact that one cannot make one's peace with God if one is not also willing to make one's peace with one's brothers.

57-83; Z. Alszeghy, "Die Theologie des Wortes Gottes bei den mittelalterlichen Theologen," in *Gregorianum* 40 (1959), pp. 671-744; D. Barsotti, *Christliches Mysterium und Wort Gottes* (Einsiedeln, 1957); K. Rahner, "The Word and the Eucharist," in *Theological Investigations* IV (London & Baltimore, 1967), pp. 253-81; O. Semmelroth, *Wirkendes Wort. Zur Theologie der Verkündigung* (Frankfurt a. M., 1962); M. Schmaus, *Wahrheit als Heilsbegegnung* (Theologische Fragen heute, I) (Munich, 1964); L. Scheffczyk, *Von der Heilsmacht des Wortes. Grundzüge einer Theologie des Wortes* (Munich, 1966).

[9] Cf. particularly St. Augustine, *Enchiridion de fide, spe et caritate*, cc. 69ff. (*P.L.*, 40, pp. 265ff.).

II

LAY CONFESSION

Ecclesiastical tradition contains many other forms of confession, among which lay confession is prominently featured. In James 5, 16-19 the apostle admonishes: "So confess your sins to one another, and pray for one another, and this will cure you; the heartfelt prayer of a good man works very powerfully. . . . My brothers, if one of you strays away from the truth, and another brings him back to it, he may be sure that anyone who can bring back a sinner from the wrong way that he has taken will be saving a soul from death and covering up a great number of sins."

Most modern exegetes do not interpret this process as belonging to sacramental confession in the strict sense, for in this case the presbyter is allotted no particular function.[10] In this case it would appear that James is encouraging lay confession. According to a community regulation mentioned in Matthew 18, 15. 18, representatives of the official Church should only step in when a discussion between two people, or one that also includes other members of the community, is unavailing. We can see, therefore, that the official form of confession through exclusion from, and then reincorporation into, the community of the Church is, as it were, the *ultima ratio,* the extraordinary rather than the ordinary means of bringing the sinner back to God and to the community.

In the early Church the entire community joined in with its intercession and penances on behalf of the sinner;[11] particular importance was accorded the intercession of martyrs and monks.[12] From these practices there developed in the early and high Middle Ages the theory and practice of lay confession.[13] It was usu-

[10] F. Mussner, *Der Jakobusbrief* (Herders Theol. Kommentar z. N.T., XIII/1) (Freiburg i. Br., 1964), pp. 226f.

[11] B. Poschmann, *op. cit.*

[12] K. Rahner, "Monchsbeichte," in *Lex. f. Theol. u. Kirche* VII, pp. 538f.

[13] On this see A. Teetaert, *La confession aux laiques dans l'Eglise latine depuis le VIIIe siècle jusqu'au XIVe siècle* (Paris & Bruges, 1926); B.

ally regarded as the ordinary means of making peace after minor sins, and as the extraordinary means of doing so after major sins in those cases where no priest was available. In such cases lay confession was normally considered to be a particularly genuine expression of the *votum sacramenti*.

Thus, Thomas Aquinas called lay confession an incomplete sacrament,[14] while Albert the Great felt justified in considering the layman dispensing forgiveness in this way *minister vicarius*, to whom the requisite authority was given on account of the Church's unity in faith and in love.[15] But he, too, maintained that these lay confessions lacked the essence of a sacrament in the fullest sense.[16]

But through Thomas Aquinas, and particularly through Duns Scotus, absolution through a priest was given such strong emphasis that lay confession became increasingly more rare until finally, through Counter-Reformation measures, a valuable tradition was lost altogether.

With the partiality of the Counter-Reformation now behind us, it would be a good thing if this form of confession were once again brought out into the open. It could be of value to parents in their relationship with their children (not infrequently they have to fill the role of what one might call a domestic priest), to a married couple within their own relationship, and between friends.

Poschmann, *Die abendländische Kirchenbusse im* frühen Mittelalter (Breslau, 1930), pp. 183-7; E. Amann and A. Michel, "Penitence," in *Dict. Théol. cath.* XII, pp. 930f., 936, 964ff., 983, 1025, 1031f.; K. Rahner, "Laienbeichte," in *Lex. f. Theol. u. Kirche* VI, pp. 741f. To reach an historically relevant assessment of the phenomenon of lay confession one should remember that until Thomas Aquinas the sacramentality question, and particularly the question of the actual significance of the priest's absolution, had not yet been explained and defined in the way in which, through Trent, we have it today. To reach further back than Aquinas is a difficult process, but this need not prevent us today from adopting those elements from the Church's tradition and getting what we can from them in the pursuit of our present discussions.

[14] St. Thomas Aquinas, *Summa theologica*, Suppl., q. 8, a. 2, ad 1 et 3.
[15] Albert the Great, IV *Sent.*, d. 17, a. 58f.
[16] *Ibid.*, a. 39. On the differentiation of Albert the Great's dual concept of sacrament, cf. P. Teetaert, *op. cit.*, p. 315; A. Michel, *loc. cit.*, p. 967.

Additionally, it might be considered for use by lay people of mature Christian spirituality and wide experience in life. In many everyday affairs lay people will be more experienced than priests. Lay confession could therefore be considered for use among the general run of everyday situations in which error occurs and spiritual guidance is needed. However, it would only be suitable in a case of real emergency in those situations where a Christian has totally severed his connection with Christ and the community of the Church (a situation that Matthew 18, 15ff. apparently presupposes), that is, when he is really living in serious sin.[17] In a case such as this the Church must act through her official representatives and administer the sacrament of penance in its strictest sense.

From what has been said, it can be seen that the essence of lay confession is made up of three elements: (1) mutual conversion, which means tactfully and wisely making one another aware of mistakes, dangers and wrong attitudes; (2) the promise of God's grace, the word of encouragement, spiritual advice, encouragement in the Christian life, incitement to good and illustrations of how the Christian life can be realized; (3) intercession for the other and representative penance (i.e., a willingness to do penance on the other's behalf). Readiness to undertake the latter would be an unambiguous way of distinguishing a self-righteous wish to criticize from a genuine *correctio fraterna* in which one is himself ready to do penance for the other.

Another type of lay confession is reconciliatory confession in which a fault is confessed to the person whom one has offended, be it in the heat of an argument, through some slanderous remark, or in any other similar way. Confession of this type needs no particular ritual to complete it—just an apology, a handshake, the verbal expression of reconciliation and a readiness in the two concerned to pray for one another (this latter need not be explicitly expressed, though it should be tacitly presupposed).

Among Christians, decent behavior such as this is always

---

[17] The differentiation between minor and major sins needs a thorough explanation, but this cannot be supplied here.

relevant to the salvation process: there can be no separation between reconciliation with the brother and reconciliation with God. There exist many difficulties and inhibitions peculiar to family and social life, in monasteries and convents and within the general to and fro of the exercise of ecclesiastical authority; these arise because this form of confession is not taken seriously or practiced. As a consequence, the tensions that evolve and intensify render the fulfilling of Christian and Church duties extremely difficult and complicated. Christ's own words make the use of this confession of reconciliation a necessary course to take before one approaches the eucharist (Mt. 5, 23ff.).

III

GENERAL CONFESSION

Practiced in this form, confession takes on a liturgical structure. It consists in a general—that is to say, a communal—confession of unspecified sins, following which the priest sacramentally administers absolution. This form of confession, of which we are presently entitled to make use only in exceptional and emergency cases,[18] has strong roots within Church tradition. The Old Testament shows that general absolution was dispensed to the assembled community,[19] and there are enough signs in the New Testament and in the writings of the earliest Church Fathers to indicate that the first Christian liturgies also knew of it.[20]

It is well known that the early Church possessed an ordered confessional liturgy.[21] By the 5th and 6th centuries we see the inclusion of the community in prayers said for penitents; what remains of this liturgy can be found today in the *Oratio super populum* during Lent.[22]

[18] On this see E. Eichmann and K. Morsdorf, *Lehrbuch des Kirchenrechts* II (Paderborn, 1953), p. 75.

[19] E. Würthwein, *op. cit.*, p. 977.

[20] Jas. 5, 16. 19f.; 1 Jn. 1, 9; 5, 16; *Didache* 4, 14; 14, 1.

[21] J. Jungmann, *Die lateinische Bussriten in ihrer geschichtlichen Entwicklung* (Innsbruck, 1932).

[22] *Ibid.*, pp. 38-44.

Likewise, the whole community soon became involved in the Maundy Thursday ceremony of the reincorporation of penitents into the Church (a ceremony that in the early Church was the essential sacramental rite of the sacrament of penance). From the 10th century onward this reconciliation service was also permitted on other days of the year.

From the 11th century onward there is increasing evidence that general absolutions of this type were frequently connected with the sermon; at the preacher's instigation the people would raise their hands, or recite the *Confiteor,* and then receive absolution. It seems, then, that the Church in those days had a type of general absolution that largely fulfilled the function of the confessional service we have today, for those involved were urged to confess their more grievous sins to a priest privately.[23]

Although, as time went on, this type of general absolution was denied its strictly sacramental character, it survived into the Middle Ages in such forms as the *Confiteor* and the day hours (Prime and Compline)[24] and right into our own century through the "open confession" that in many places succeeded the Sunday sermon.[25]

In both cases we are considering a "rudimentary" confessional liturgy. It is a great shame that the liturgical renewal has done so very little about their last remains; not only has it failed to renew them but it has almost totally destroyed their last traces. To this day the Eastern Church has maintained the sacramental forgiveness of sins through the general absolution as an acceptable form of confession outside the confessional,[26] and the Protestant liturgy has preserved at least the general admission of guilt, with the celebrant's prayer of intercession as a conclusion to the ceremony.[27]

Dissatisfaction with current confessional practice—particularly

[23] *Ibid.,* pp. 275-95.
[24] *Idem, The Mass of the Roman Rite* (New York, 1950), pp. 299ff.
[25] *Ibid.,* pp. 490-4.
[26] J.-H. Dalmais, "Le sacrement de pénitence chez les Orientaux," in *Maison-Dieu* 56 (1958), pp. 22-9.
[27] For example, *Agende für die evangelische Kirche der Union* I (Witten, 1959), pp. 153ff.

when great hordes of people queue for confession before a feast day, necessitating the sausage machine process we have come to know so well—has once again raised the question of reintroducing general confession within the framework of a confession liturgy as a matter for urgent consideration within the Catholic Church.[28]

Such a liturgy could be made up as follows: scripture reading, hymns and/or psalms, homily, wisely-phrased confessional questions to which each person must answer for himself before God, a communal confession of fault, possibly an offertory procession and, finally, the sacramental administration of absolution through prayer while the priest extends his hands over the congregation.

However, the introduction of such a ceremony should not lead to the demise or devaluation of individual private confession. For truly major sins this should remain as obligatory as it is now, and it also has a role to play in those cases where someone is in need of spiritual guidance.[29] Indeed, the reintroduction of a confession liturgy could so remove the pressure from the confession box that priests would at last be able to use the sacrament for the exercise of the function for which one most recommends it.

In general, perhaps the form of confession I have just outlined, provided the sermon and the questions were wisely handled, could in its own fashion contribute to the development of conscience quite as well as does the private confession at present. Its structure would lend a much stronger emphasis to the community character of the sacrament and would arouse in the participants the spirit of intercessionary and vicarious penance. Finally, one should not overlook the fact that one would be re-presenting a piece of early Church tradition in a form appropriate to our times. In the same spirit of deference to tradition, it would clearly be most appropriate if the ceremony were to be carried out dur-

---

[28] Cf. *supra,* footnote 3.

[29] K. Rahner, "Vom Sinn der häufigen Andachtsbeichte," in *Schriften zur Theologie* III (Einsiedeln, 1956), pp. 211-26 (the translation of this book, *Theological Investigations* III, is in preparation). H. Meyer, *op. cit.,* points out the dangers in an unduly close connection between the sacrament of penance and spiritual guidance.

ing those periods in the Church's year traditionally assigned for the purpose in the early Church—namely, Advent, Lent, major vigils and the ember days.

Meanwhile, for as long as a confessional liturgy with sacramental absolution is not permitted, one without it would be perfectly possible, although it should include the priest's prayer of intercession. In many cases it might well be an acceptable substitute for the purely devotional form of private confession (i.e., where in fact no grievous sin is confessed). It could also be used as a form of communal preparation for confession coupled with the opportunity for those participating to have their confession heard privately there and then, although obviously, for such an exercise to be effective, there would have to be several priests present.

Of course, I do not pretend that the introduction of these practical reforms would settle the dogmatic questions presently keeping the Churches at variance on this issue. Such questions hinge basically on the nature of ministry, a problem that needs thorough discussion in its own right. But our differences also rest upon the differentiation between sacramental and non-sacramental (that is, not fully sacramental) confession. Without going into this issue here, it should be noted that to assess this difference in quantitative terms, or in those of the assuredness of grace in one case as against another, would be to misunderstand disastrously what is at stake. It may well be that some Catholics actively entertain magical sacramental notions of this type, but it is certainly not the Church's teaching. The difference lies not in the quantity of grace, for this God grants as he wills and with regard to the needs of the personal faith of the penitent, but in the manner in which the grace of reconciliation is granted, and in the specific, Christian and human situation in which God's mercy is promulgated.

In its strictest sense the sacrament of penance exists primarily to remedy the situation of a man in grievous sin (a most unusual situation for a practicing Christian to be in) who has decisively separated himself from God and from the Church community.

But on this side of that extreme situation Christian life finds room for many different stages and degrees of intensity. In her confessional practice, too, the Church can only do justice to this dynamic and pilgrim-like character of Christian life and to the differing levels of expression within its permissible pluralism when she allows for various forms of it and remains adaptable and sensitive in thought and deed.

In becoming all this she creates a primary and indispensable condition for the meaningful discussion of the thorny questions that still remain. Only when the Church has made full use of the riches of her own tradition in the matter of confession will she be in a position to speak about the structure and theology of those of other Churches; only then will we be able to do justice to the pastoral needs that face us today.

David Stanley, S.J./*Willowdale, Canada*

Ecumenically Significant Aspects of New Testament Eucharistic Doctrine

I t is becoming abundantly clear that if the ecumenical dialogue between Christians has increased our awareness of the extent to which we profess the same faith, it has also impressed upon many of the participants the urgent necessity of reexamining those doctrinal points which divide us in order to avoid the very real danger of relativism in doctrine. One area in which such reexamination is imperative is that of the interpretation of the New Testament data relative to the eucharist. A little over a year and a half ago Paul VI's encyclical *Mysterium fidei,* concentrating as it avowedly did upon only a few facets of Catholic eucharistic teaching, evoked varying reactions both within and outside the Catholic Church. The pope's concern was directed to certain trends in modern Catholic theological thought and practice which he felt might undermine the ancient orthodox faith in the eucharist. Hence, he restricted himself to a restatement of the traditional Catholic position concerning the sacrificial character of the Mass, the continuing relevance of the term "transubstantiation", the real presence and the importance for Christian piety of devotion to the reserved sacrament.

It is surely obvious that *Mysterium fidei* did not provide a complete summary of Catholic eucharistic teaching. Such was not Pope Paul's intention. It did, however, touch some sensitive questions of vital importance to the newer phase of ecumenical discussion. The purpose of the present article is to reconsider four aspects of New Testament eucharistic teaching, passed over by *Mysterium fidei,* in order to make some little contribution to the second stage of ecumenical exchange: the candid presentation of how we interpret the scriptural evidence. We wish to examine what the New Testament says about the character of the eucharist as meal, as proclamation, as memorial and as thanksgiving.

I

THE EUCHARIST AS MEAL

If we examine the descriptions of eucharistic celebrations in the apostolic age that are given in the New Testament, we find that the meal aspect is their most basic and common characteristic. The author of Acts refers to the eucharist as "the breaking of the bread". Thus he depicts the primitive Jerusalem community as "being devoted to the teaching of the apostles and the common life, the breaking of the bread and prayers" (Acts 2, 42). A few lines further on we read that these Christians "were faithful to daily attendance at the Temple in a group, while, breaking bread at home, they partook of the food with great joy and simplicity of heart" (v. 46). The Temple liturgy for these Jewish Christians continued to be regarded as public worship; the eucharist was, however, the focal point of their specifically Christian lives. This rite was characterized by joy, for the first disciples had retained, as the Gospel traditions testify (Lk. 24, 30-35. 41-43; Acts 1, 4; Jn. 21, 9-13), a vivid recollection of how frequently the risen Lord Jesus had come to them in connection with a meal. Moreover, the summary to which we refer (Acts 2, 42-47) indicates that it was the "breaking of the bread" which preserved and deepened in these first Christians the sense of community. It is scarcely accidental that between the two references to the eucharist (v. 42 and v. 46) we find the statement that "they possessed everything in common: they sold their property and possessions, and distributed the proceeds to all in accordance with each one's needs" (vv. 44-45). This practice of communal living was motivated by the eucharist.

At a later period, the meal character of the eucharist was still prominent, as may be gathered from the narrative of Paul's visit to Troas, which records a Sunday celebration of "the breaking of bread", accompanied by an instruction to the community (Acts 20, 7-12). Paul's own description of the eucharistic observance at Corinth indicates that it formed an integral part of a meal, whose chief purpose was to promote the feeling of solidarity within that Church. As the chief remedy for the divisive factors threatening Christian unity in Corinth, Paul insisted upon the proper conduct of the community meal, at which each member of the Church was expected to share his food with others (1 Cor. 11, 17ff.). This common supper was designed to come to a climax in the eucharist, from which it derived its name as "the Lord's supper" (v. 20). It was precisely because the abuses that had crept in were undermining the veritable meal character of this whole ritual that the apostle manifested such concern and warned offenders of the impending divine judgment (vv. 27-34).

The nearest the New Testament comes to connecting this eucharistic meal with sacrifice is the passage in which Paul compares it with the sacrificial meals prescribed by the Mosaic ritual and with the sacral banquets held in pagan temples, whereby those who had offered sacrifice were thought to become table companions of the gods (1 Cor. 10, 18-21). The fact that Paul has just spoken of the eucharist as a sharing, first in the blood, then in the body of Christ, serves (in the opinion of many commentators) to heighten this sacrificial character. "The cup of blessing which we bless, is it not participation in the blood of Christ? The bread which we break, is it not participation in the body of Christ?" (v. 16). Still, Thomas Barrosse is probably correct in his judgment that "Paul's assimilation of the eucharist to Jewish *thysiai* seems based on the similar effects of eating the eucharist and the *thysiai* rather than on any desire to affirm the sacrificial character of the Christian rite".[1]

The scriptural evidence we have reviewed compels the conclusion that in the apostolic age the eucharist was habitually thought of as a meal, symbolizing that fellowship essential to the Christian life. Yet, the same evidence indicates that it was believed to be a meal which had acquired a totally new significance. Other symbols of the sense of community (the sharing of goods in Jerusalem, the sharing of victuals in Corinth) could and did change. In fact, their effectiveness as symbols derived from their connection with the eucharist's *sacramental* symbolism. This totally new significance of the eucharistic meal is asserted by Paul. "Because there is one loaf, we though many are one body, since we all share in the one loaf" (1 Cor. 10, 17). The point of departure for this profound insight is the obvious symbolism of the single loaf. Paul's thought, however, quickly moves to another plane, for he is aware that the consecrated loaf *is* in reality the glorified body of Christ which has the power to unify the community through its participation in this unique meal.

The discourse on the bread of life in the fourth gospel underscores even more emphatically the totally new meaning (the sacramental value) of eating this "bread of life", which Jesus promises. His flesh and blood are indeed "real" (*alēthēs*) food and drink (Jn. 6, 55); yet the meal at which they are consumed imparts "eternal life" (v. 54). The evangelist has already pointed out the cause of this astonishing truth by citing, in terms peculiar to himself, Jesus' words of institution at the Last Supper: "And the bread which I will give—it is my flesh for the life of the world" (Jn. 6, 51). This Johannine version of the words of consecration, no less than the sayings found in the Synoptics, indicates Jesus' redemptive death as a source of the life-giving power of the eucharist. For in Johannine theology, that death is the beginning of Jesus' glorification, completed by his resurrection and

---

[1] T. Barrosse, "The Eucharist: Sacrifice and Meal? An Examination of the New Testament Data," in *Yearbook of Liturgical Studies* (1966), p. 74.

ascension, through which he is empowered to give the Holy Spirit (Jn. 7, 39). John does not permit his reader to forget that it is the glorified Christ who is present in the eucharist, imparting the Spirit who bestows "eternal life". This is the reason for the remark, so frequently misunderstood: "The Spirit is the lifegiver: the flesh is useless" (Jn. 6, 63). Holy as was the mortal flesh which the Word of God assumed at the incarnation, it was capable of imparting life to those who feed upon it only after Jesus was glorified.

Ultimately, the reason for the New Testament presentation of the eucharist as a meal goes back to the Last Supper. A striking proof that the apostolic Church believed she was faithful to Jesus' command to "do this as a remembrance of me" (Lk. 22, 19; 1 Cor. 11, 24-25) may be seen in the literary form employed by Mark[2] and Matthew[3] to record Jesus' essential words and actions on this sacred occasion. It seems fairly certain that both these evangelists inserted into their narratives of the Last Supper eucharistic liturgical formulas that were current in the communities to which they belonged or for which they wrote their gospels. By this technique these evangelists testify that what the Church performed at her central act of public worship was what Jesus himself had done at the Last Supper.

At the Last Supper, the apostolic Church believed—as these liturgical texts in Mark and Matthew, together with the Lucan (Lk. 22, 15-20) and Pauline (1 Cor. 11, 23-25) accounts attest —Jesus intended his words and gestures over the bread and wine to be taken as referring to his redemptive death. He indicated his body as "given on your behalf" (Lk. 22, 19; cf. Jn. 6, 51; 1 Cor. 11, 24), and his blood as "being poured out on behalf of the many unto remission of sins" (Mt. 26, 28; cf. Mk. 14, 24; Lk. 15, 20). More important still was Jesus' designation of his blood as "testament blood" (Mk., Mt.), which Paul and Luke explicitate as "the new testament in my blood". Thus Jesus associated what

---

[2] P. Benoit, "Les récits de l'institution de l'eucharistie et leur portée," in *Exégèse et Théologie* I (1961), p. 212.

[3] D. Stanley, *The Gospel of St. Matthew* (Collegeville, 1963), p. 109.

he did at the Last Supper with his self-oblation on Calvary as the inauguration of the "new covenant" announced by Jeremiah (Jer. 31, 31ff.). It is this association which gives its sacrificial significance to the celebration of the eucharist.[4] The instrument of covenant-making was his body and blood, given for men under the appearance of bread and wine at the Last Supper, and upon the cross at Calvary. As Dom Jacques Dupont has shown, it is this designation of the eucharist as the instrument of the New Covenant which best demonstrates the real presence of Christ in the eucharist.[5]

II

THE EUCHARIST AS MEMORIAL AND PROCLAMATION

As we have already noted, Paul and Luke explicitly record Jesus' command to repeat what he did at the Last Supper "in remembrance of me". Mark and Matthew imply the injunction by their borrowing from the liturgy, by which the apostolic Church carried out this last injunction of Jesus. This act of remembering, however, was not regarded simply as a recall through a purely symbolic action of an event whose reality remained totally in the past, a matter of history. To think of it in this way is to ignore the profound realism with which the bible regards the annual "remembrance" or memorial (Ex. 12, 14) of Israel's deliverance from Egypt and the covenant which Yahweh made with her. That the passover rite constituted annually a contemporary event may be gathered from the words which the Deuteronomist, writing several centuries after the exodus from Egypt, addressed to his contemporaries: "Yahweh our God made a covenant *with us* at Horeb. It was not with our ancestors that Yahweh made this covenant, but with ourselves, those of us who are *all here alive today*" (Dt. 5, 2-3). Johannes Behm has rightly de-

[4] P. Benoit, "The Holy Eucharist," in *Scripture* 8 (1956), pp. 102-4.
[5] J. Dupont, "Ceci est mon corps—Ceci est mon sang," in *Nouv. Rev. Théol.* 80 (1958), pp. 1025-41.

scribed the purpose of the eucharistic *anamnēsis* as "the making present by the later community of the Lord who instituted the Supper and who through his death made the new covenant a reality. . . ." [6] Pierre Benoit concurs: "It is not simply a commemoration of a departed friend . . . but the renewal of a sacred action by which the sacrifice of the undying Master is made present through the bread and wine." [7]

However, Paul's own comment on this command of our Lord provides the best clue to its meaning: "As often as you eat this bread and drink from the cup, you proclaim the death of the Lord until he comes" (1 Cor. 11, 26). Three points are to be noted: the action is classified as a proclamation, whose content is the death of the Lord, and whose orientation is to the parousia. The word "proclaim" is a technical term in Paul (and in Acts) for the preaching of the Good News of salvation through Jesus' death and resurrection (cf. Phil. 1, 17; 1 Cor. 2, 1; Col. 1, 28, etc.). The event-quality of the apostolic preaching is seen in the *metanoia,* or conversion to Christian faith, which is its principal aim. To speak of the eucharist as proclamation is to insist upon it as the sacramental reenactment of "the death of *the Lord*", that is, of the glorified Christ. It is through the real presence of the risen Lord that his death becomes a present reality in the eucharist. Paul was as fully aware as was the author of the Apocalypse that the glorified Christ is what he now is by reason of his entire past history, including his passion. In the Apocalypse this truth is presented dramatically by characterizing Christ, the Lord of history, as "the lamb that has been slain" (cf. Apoc. 5, 6 *et passim*). Paul's phrase "until he comes" indicates something more than the termination of the enactment of the eucharist. This sacred meal, celebrated by the Christian community as it awaits the second coming, was thought of as an anticipation of the parousia through the real sacramental presence of the exalted Christ.

---

[6] J. Behm, "Anamnēsis, Hypomnēsis," in *Theol. Wörterb. z. N.T.* I, pp. 351-2.

[7] P. Benoit, "The Holy Eucharist," in *Scripture* 8 (1956), p. 106.

III

THE EUCHARIST AS THANKSGIVING

The term "eucharist" is not used in the New Testament to denominate this sacrament (except in the poorly attested variant for "the cup of blessing": 1 Cor. 10, 16). In the narratives of institution, the term *eucharistein* ("give thanks") is used as a synonym for *eulogein* ("bless"). In biblical usage, to thank or bless God for his bountiful works of salvation is a form of divine praise. More specifically, as a description of Jesus' action at the Last Supper, it probably refers to his "grace" or blessing over the food. After the analogy of the Jewish *berakah,* this prayer of Jesus undoubtedly made reference to God's great saving deeds, of which his own approaching death was to be the climax. Whether or not Jesus actually celebrated the passover ritual at the Last Supper, the allusions to this rite in the Synoptic narratives (especially in that of Luke)[8] surely indicate that the apostolic Church understood the eucharist to be the prophetic fulfillment of this ancient Israelite feast. Jesus, by instituting the Christian sacrament, was simply bringing to its culmination the long development which the passover supper had undergone in the course of history.[9]

The awareness of the early Church that "the breaking of the bread" was essentially an act of grateful praise of God for his supreme act of redemption in Jesus Christ accounts for the joyous note which, as we have seen, characterized the eucharist from the earliest days. The designation of this central act of Christian worship as "thanksgiving" underscores its essentially paschal and festive character which, according to the recent *Constitution on the Sacred Liturgy,* must always make itself felt, even in the Lenten liturgy and in Masses of requiem.

    [8] P. Benoit, "Le récit de la cène en Luc XXII," in *Exégèse et Théologie* I (1961), pp. 164-209.
    [9] C. Stuhlmueller, "Old Testament Liturgy," in *Studies in Salvation History,* ed. C. Luke Salm (Englewood Cliffs, 1964), pp. 81-91.

John Meyendorff / *New York, N. Y.*

Notes on the Orthodox Understanding of the Eucharist

I

THE CONTROVERSY—PAST AND PRESENT

The Middle Ages saw the appearance of a profusion of "lists of heresies" thrown mutually at each other by the Latins and the Greeks. Problems connected with the eucharist occupy a prominent place in those lists, especially since the conflict between Patriarch Michael Cerularius and Cardinal Humbert in 1054. The question of the bread used in the sacrament—whether it should be leavened or unleavened—was, for example, considered throughout the 14th and 15th centuries to be a major doctrinal divergence between the two Churches.

It is obvious that no one will adopt the same attitude today: the medieval disputes between Latins and Greeks, especially those of the 11th and 12th centuries, were disputes of rubricists, and they implicitly acknowledged that a simple adjustment of rubrics could bring the Churches back together. Paradoxically, the very futility of the Greco-Latin debates of that period supposed that the schism did not exist "in depth". The really great theologians, Photius, for example, were able to bring the two parties to forget human "traditions" and to achieve unity on the basis of the one holy tradition of the Catholic Church.[1] Even

---

[1] "Everybody must preserve what was defined by common ecumenical decisions," wrote Photius to Pope Nicholas I, "but a particular opinion of

today, the seriousness of the ecumenical dialogue depends upon our common concern for the true, catholic dimensions of the issues under discussion.

The eucharistic liturgy is the point when the essential redemptive act of Christ is realized for us—the "re-union" with God of fallen humanity and the "recapitulation" of humanity in its original unity, now restored in Jesus Christ. A solution to the difficulties between Orthodox and Roman Catholics in the issue of the eucharist can therefore only be given in the light of soteriology. For obviously, if the divergences in forms and in rubrics were brought about by separate—and generally legitimate—historical developments, and can therefore be tolerated and often encouraged as mutually enriching forms of a single tradition, the theological differences in understanding salvation are more difficult to bridge. These differences have, in turn, influenced liturgical ritual and sometimes given to accidental and formal aspects of the liturgy a totally new significance.

II

ANAMNESIS AND EPICLESIS

Let us take three examples, the first being the famous issue of the relation, in the framework of the eucharistic canon, between the "anamnesis" and the "epiclesis". As is well known, the *anamnesis,* i.e., the account of the event of the Last Supper, containing the words of institution—"This is my body"; "This is my blood" —is considered in the Latin West as the sacramental "formula" through which the priest, acting *in persona Christi,* performs

---

a Church Father or a definition issued by a local council can be followed by some and ignored by others." From the context of the letter, it is obvious that the patriarch has in view liturgical and disciplinary divergences. He concludes: "When the faith remains inviolate, the common and catholic decisions are also safe; a sensible man respects the practices and laws of others" (*Ep.* 2: *P.G.* 102, 604D-605D. Other Byzantine theologians have expressed similar views on liturgical diversity; cf. my book, *Orthodoxy and Catholicity,* (New York: Sheed and Ward, 1966), pp. 97-101; on Photius, see F. Dvornik, *The Photian Schism* (London, 1948).

the sacrament. The canon of the Roman Mass—as well as, for that matter, of the Anglican eucharist—supposes in its present form precisely this type of sacramental theology. While not necessarily being a product of a juridical soteriology based upon the notions of "merit" and "satisfaction", the present Roman rite is perfectly suited for it, and the Western Middle Ages developed a piety for which the Mass was only an expression of the Anselmian doctrine of redemption. Meanwhile, all the Eastern forms of the liturgy, while also containing the *anamnesis,* follow it by an invocation of the Holy Spirit:

"We pray you," says the priest, ". . . send down your Holy Spirit upon us and upon these gifts, and make this bread—the precious body of your Christ—and that which is in this cup—the precious blood of your Christ—making the change by your Holy Spirit" (Liturgy of Chrysostom).

The Eastern *epiclesis* solemnly proclaims, on the one hand, that the restoration of unity between God and man is a trinitarian action. For the presence of Christ in the community, the action of the Holy Spirit is not only essential; it is implied by the very trinitarian life of God, in which humanity is introduced. And actually all traditional sacramental prayers—especially that of the baptismal initiation, of which the sacrament of confirmation is a part—include, at their very central point, an invocation of the Spirit. On the other hand, the eucharistic act is a *prayer*. The notion of the bishop or priest, acting through the *anamnesis* as an image of Christ, is not excluded by the *epiclesis,* but the dimension and significance of his role are fulfilled only in the *prayer* he pronounces in the name of the congregation, asking the Spirit to abide "upon us and upon these gifts", and to "make the change. . . ."

The presence of the *epiclesis* in the eucharistic canon is therefore more than a simple liturgical detail. In anti-Latin polemics, many Orthodox authors have argued in favor of it, by trying to visualize it as the "Orthodox formula of consecration", as opposed to the Latin one found in the words of institution. However, because it is also a *prayer,* the *epiclesis* excludes the very idea that sacraments are performed simply "when the correct formula is pronounced with the right intention by the rightly appointed minister". To invoke the Holy Spirit at the eucharist is not simply another sacramental "formula":[2] it implies a doctrine of salvation and an ecclesiology.

The task of the Church is to actualize the redemptive act of Christ *for us*—i.e., to offer us sanctification, of which the Spirit, whom the Son sends from the Father, is the agent. This sanctification is never achieved automatically or magically; it has to be accepted freely by man, for "where the Spirit of the Lord is, there is freedom" (2 Cor. 3, 17), and the Church is precisely the place where this free acceptance of God's grace by man becomes possible. In the Church, the antinomy between divine power and human free will is solved by their "cooperation" (the *synergeia* of the Greek Fathers). The eucharistic *epiclesis* realizes this central soteriological and ecclesiological notion which closely corresponds to the entire Greek patristic understanding of salvation: divine grace and participation in divine life are restored in man when he turns *freely* to God. Thus "grace" and "natural freedom" are not mutually exclusive, but suppose each other.[3]

Western sacramental theology since the Middle Ages, but especially since the Counter-Reformation, has been dominated by a concern for defining sacramental "validity" in itself. In the East, the notion of "validity" remained very closely linked with ecclesiology. No one in the Orthodox Church will ever doubt that the invocation of the Holy Spirit, solemnly pronounced in the eucharistic liturgy by the celebrant in the name of the whole Church, is being answered by God. However, the very fact that it is a *prayer* and an *invocation* supposes that "to be the Church" requires a free effort of the congregation to be in the fullness of truth, in fullness of communion with the Catholic tradition. There is no external guarantee that a given local community is truly "the Church" unless it opens itself to the guidance of the Spirit of

[2] Cf. Archimandrite Kiprian, *Evkharistiya* (Paris, 1947), p. 284.
[3] This well-known patristic notion of "freedom through participation" is well emphasized by V. Lossky in James Clarke's *The Mystical Theology of the Eastern Church* (London, 1957), pp. 197ff.

Truth. The *epiclesis* proclaims this opening, and the presence of Christ in the sacrament is God's answer which truly causes the Church to be the Church. The Church's permanence and the objective reality of the sacrament are then based on God's promise to be "with his own" forever.

The sacramental theology implied by the centrality of the *epiclesis* in the eucharistic canon is therefore obviously and closely connected with the patristic doctrine of salvation and is quite independent from the problematics which dominated the West in the Reformation and Counter-Reformation periods.

III

ECCLESIOLOGICAL DIMENSION OF THE EUCHARIST

The second example that we would like to discuss concerns the ecclesiological dimension of the eucharist. The Orthodox insistence on the fundamental "identity" of all local Churches is based on the idea that in the eucharist the Church really becomes the Church of God. "Where Christ Jesus is, there is the Catholic Church," wrote St. Ignatius of Antioch:[4] the presence of Christ in the community determines the quality of the body. An assembly of human beings then becomes the body of Christ, the entire body, not a part of it, for even those absent, the Virgin Mary, the saints and the departed are united in the catholic reality of *each* eucharist, which thus becomes precisely the Church of God in a given place.

Normally, a eucharistic assembly is presided over by a bishop, and this "norm", as is well known, corresponded to actual practice in the early Church. The division of the local Church or episcopal "diocese" into several "parishes", each presided over by a presbyter, was determined by historical circumstances of the 2nd and 3rd centuries. It somehow obscured the original relationship between the eucharist and the Church.[5] The power of

[4] *Epistle to the Smyrnaeans*, 8, 2.
[5] This problem has recently been very ably discussed by J. Zizioulas, *E henotes tes ecclesias* (Athens, 1965).

the bishop, in particular, began to function independently from and above the sacramental reality of the eucharist. However, the primitive eucharistic dimension of the episcopal function was preserved in Canon Law and the principles of ecclesiastical organization. The Orthodox opposition to the papacy—i.e., to the notion that one of the bishops would have *jure divino* a power extending beyond the membership of his own local Church (or diocese) and *over* the other bishops who possess the same sacramental function in their respective Churches as he does in his own—is based upon the idea that jurisdictional and sacramental powers are fundamentally inseparable.

The unity of the bishops among themselves is founded upon the mutual recognition of the identity of their episcopate— *"Episcopatus unus est,"* wrote St. Cyprian[6]—and the unity of all local Churches upon the identity of their faith, and not upon their common obedience to an "extra-eucharistic" center. The existence of a universal primacy and of various regional primacies is certainly not excluded by this ecclesiology, but their nature is determined by the requirements of the mission of the Church in the world; they are therefore essentially relative to this mission. The Church cannot exist without them, but they can never determine the Church's nature.[7]

The relationship between the eucharist and the doctrine of the Church has recently gained a new emphasis in Orthodox theology. When pushed to the extreme, this emphasis tends to oppose, somehow artificially, the notions of "eucharistic ecclesiology" and "universal ecclesiology", and denies Christian validity to the latter, as if the Church had no "universal" existence and "universal" mission. However, if one takes exception to those exaggerations, the full realization that the local Church is not a "part" of the body, but the body in its entirety and wholeness, is a necessary dimension of Orthodox ecclesiology which modern "eucharistic" ecclesiology has helped to clarify.

---

[6] *De Catholicae Ecclesiae Unitate,* 5.
[7] Cf. J. Meyendorff, N. Afanassieff, A. Schmemann, N. Koulomzine, *The Primacy of Peter in the Orthodox Church* (London: The Faith Press, 1963).

IV

THE PROBLEM OF SACRAMENTAL INTERCOMMUNION

Consideration of the theological and ecclesiological dimensions of the eucharist leads us, finally, to the third issue which was raised by the *Decree on Ecumenism* of Vatican Council II: the problem of sacramental "intercommunion" between separated Christian bodies, and in particular between the Roman Catholics and the Orthodox. The Council's attitude in this question, opening, at least partially, the door to "intercommunion", was based essentially upon the recognition of "valid orders" in the Orthodox Church; meanwhile, as we have already shown, Orthodox ecclesiology, precisely because of its "eucharistic" dimension, precludes the notion of validity *per se*. It is impossible for us to say simply that sacramental presence is created by "valid orders", for the sacramental presence of Christ in the community of the Church implies not only that, but also truth, catholicity, unity, or at least the formal acceptance of the tradition of the Church in its fullness.[8] In other words, there cannot be any "validity" outside of the *one Church;* there cannot be any separation between the sacramental power of the bishops and their magisterium. Meanwhile, the Vatican decrees specify on the one hand that the Orthodox bishops have "valid priesthood" (cf., for example, the *Decree on the Catholic Churches of the Eastern Rite,* n. 25) and thus "encourage" intercommunion with them within certain disciplinary limits (*Decree on Ecumenism,* Ch. III), but these decrees also clearly state that Orthodox bishops have no doctrinal authority whatever due to their separation from the See of Rome (*Constitution on the Church,* n. 22). The logical conclusion seems to be that Catholics can partake of the sacrament in an Orthodox Church, but should avoid listening to the sermon, since the teaching delivered there is disconnected from the authentic apostolic magisterium.

[8] This has always been the general attitude of the Orthodox in relation to the recognition of Anglican orders in particular (even if some individual or local Orthodox statements may have given the impression of admitting a validity *per se*). It has been reiterated at the recent Pan-Orthodox Conference in Belgrade (September, 1966).

In Orthodox eyes, this attitude implies a theology of the eucharist which disconnects sacramental presence, an almost "magical" presence *per se,* from the fullness of life, truth and unity in Christ and the Holy Spirit.

Meanwhile, the true theological meaning of the eucharist consists precisely in manifesting this fullness and witnessing to its given reality in the Church.

Orthodox and Catholics both agree that Christ's presence in his Church is full and real, and their agreement on this point is a precious ecumenical fact. The tragedy of the schism, however, is that we do not yet agree on the content and presuppositions of this fullness. As long as this disagreement exists, any "intercommunion" would necessarily be based on a minimalistic reduction of catholicity to the notion of an abstract "validity" or, even worse, on the assumption that the fullness is not already *given* in the Church. In that case, we would both—Orthodox and Romans—become Protestants. The Orthodox opposition to "intercommunion" therefore proceeds neither from any reactionary conservatism nor from lack of ecumenical concern. It simply tries to preserve the notion that true Christian unity is a *God-made* reality, that it is based upon the common acceptance of Christ's truth as *he* wants it to be accepted, and that this is precisely what happens in the eucharist.

If we participate in it together now, in the midst of our divisions, we would implicitly, but blasphemously, accept them as tolerable. This would be the very opposite of true ecumenism.

Renzo Bertalot/ *Venice, Italy*

Understanding Protestant Teaching on the Lord's Supper

P resent-day ecumenical encounters must constantly keep in mind the eucharistic perspective which, because of our divisions, is complex, but will become simpler on the day willed by the Lord. Accordingly, we can today become aware of the great difficulties with which the path of Christian theology is strewn and the fact that the notion of faith is determined by an internal dynamic tension between confessional and eschatological obligation.

Difficulty of Confrontation

In approaching the more important problems of an ecumenical confrontation on the eucharist, we discover that the matter is much more extensive. We must clear up the working bases of a large number of other sectors before arriving at what interests us. Within the confessional sphere itself, many obstacles seem to have been removed and the general makeup of the problem appears well defined in its exegetical, philosophical and dogmatic components. But as soon as we prolong our gaze and seek to understand the positions of other Christian spokesmen, many affirmations inevitably and immediately become matter for discussion once again.

There is no consensus on the attempt to reconstruct linguistically the specific words used by the Lord at the institution of the sacrament. Above all, there is no consensus in establishing the meaning of the terms *body* and *blood*. For some they must be preserved with rigorous integrity, while for others they are to be reduced—not out of relativistic motives but out of motives of scientific research on the dates of the New Testament—to the sign of the person of Christ.

The same verb *to be,* which refers the bread to the body and the wine to the blood, can be interpreted—with a real biblical basis—in various and divergent ways, sometimes emphasizing a substantial evaluation and at other times a symbolic one. Naturally, these difficulties and divergences become multiplied in accord with the meaning we intend to give to the Hebraic content of the Last Supper.

As soon as we leave the biblical level and listen to the testimony of those who have preceded us in the Christian faith over the centuries, it becomes evident that decisive philosophical factors come into play. Indeed, it has been pointed out that St. Thomas' notion of substance in its Aristotelian coloring must not be confused with the one held by the Thomist Cajetan. Toward the end of the Scholastic period, the latter notion assumed a character more physical than metaphysical. The Council of Trent and the Reformation formulated their dogmatic positions in this philosophical climate which did not always favor clarification within the Western Church.[1]

Today distances have doubtless not been bridged. Confessional isolation and the diverse sensitivities in the choice of philosophical categories have contributed to a more profound indication of the lines of demarcation between Catholics and Protestants. A simple participation in present-day ecumenical encounters will be sufficient to demonstrate the difficulties of vocabulary. One must often attempt to translate what one thinks is the terminology of the other in order to be understood and to understand. The usual linguistic schemas no longer hold good in the study of

[1] H. Chavannes, "La présence réelle chez saint Thomas et chez Calvin," in *Verbum Caro* 50 (1959), p. 166.

other Christian confessions, and it is urgent to introduce a radical revision in them.

Besides language, we find ourselves confronted with working bases that carry a suspicion of prejudice even if we wish to be free from it. There is little doubt that we must labor with fear and trepidation. Therefore, it would be very important in the area of the eucharist to undertake common *research* which could give guarantees of not being transformed into a tendentious thesis—that is, one which proves something already understood. The *Decree on Ecumenism* is no stranger to these same preoccupations and desires.

The Real Presence

In his ecumenical effort to find a Protestant consensus on the celebration of the Lord's supper, Calvin held that insistence should be placed on the real presence of Christ without pausing to explain the manner in which such a presence takes place; he called this a "great mystery".[2] This might have appeared to be an unsatisfactory proposal. However, it is a fact that it represented the means whereby unity with the Zwinglian wing was achieved at the very period of the Reformation.

The ecumenical conferences of the last forty years have made good use of Calvin's suggestion to affirm their unity in diversity. This was also true of the Conference on Faith and Order held at Montreal, Canada in 1963. It specifies the magnitude of the agreement reached, notwithstanding perduring differences, but does not offer further specifications concerning the mode of the real presence of the Lord. I do not believe that such a manner of acting can be included in the framework of what is usually considered an easy compromise. If it were to be so understood, it would not be acceptable to the Church of Vatican Council II; it would not do justice to Calvin, and could not seriously be brought to the attention of the whole of Christianity. Rather, we must ask ourselves if such silence—instead of being the silence

[2] M. Thurian, *L'Eucharistie* (Neuchâtel, 1959), p. 267, footnote 28.

of witnesses who hesitate to speak—is not part of that prudent
manner of acting in the presence of God's revelation.

In all sectors of Christianity the term *mystery* is spoken of at
any given moment of confessional witnessing. Today, what seems
to lie behind Calvin's conciliatory suggestion is the different
placement of the *mystery* in the interpretative logical process.
It was usual to pass from the biblical datum to its interpretation,
locating the mystery within the latter. According to Calvin's
specifications, which were accepted by the ecumenical conferences, the mystery is more conscientiously to be referred to the
reality itself, before which every interpretation must of necessity
remain humble. In other words, the mystery governs the presence
of Christ in the supper and not in our confessional interpretation
of such a presence.

Truth and Formulation of Truth

The above reflections enable us to prolong our discussion with
the hope that the Catholic camp will accord ever wider acceptance to Pope John's distinction between truth and the formulation
of truth, which was so significantly announced at the beginning
of the work of Vatican Council II. We recall having seen—
though only from the outside—this formula animate and advance
the liturgical renewal and become part of some important directives of the *Decree on Ecumenism.*

On the other hand, we note certain Catholic precautions that
manifest themselves, above all, in the eucharistic sphere. In the
aftermath of the encyclical *Mysterium fidei,* it is clear that Pope
John's formula cannot conceivably be held today as the only one
to be adopted in the various fields of Roman theology. Yet, if
we, with the aim of contributing to the ecumenical dialogue,
must express one desire concerning an argument that has been
so much discussed, I believe it is possible to hope that Pope
John's formula will find a way to foster studies on this theme
within Catholicism. For it would be very useful, ecumenically
speaking, to be able to arrive together at a greater understanding
of the limits between truth and the formulation of truth, and the

relationship existing between the various formulations and the numerous material differences.

Sacrament

It would be difficult to separate these notes from their necessarily introductory character, since the subject itself requires it. However, in seeking to circumscribe in great extent the argument of the Last Supper, it would be useful to dwell on the notion of sacrament. The common recognition of baptism should encourage scholarly research for a consensus on the notion of sacrament. At least two types of difficulties must be faced, and they become ever more evident in the course of mixed study-meetings.

First of all, there is a different manner of appraising the *promise* and the *freedom* of God in the Church. From the outside, it seems that the promise of God plays such a role in Catholic theology as to exclude the eventuality of an unsuccessful divine intervention. In Protestantism, on the contrary, there is no hesitation about speaking of the *freedom* of God as a notion necessarily parallel to that of *promise*. Emphasis is often placed on the silence of God, the absence of God and the abandonment of God—recalling the Lord's words on the cross and the practice of fasting in the early Church.

There is not merely the awareness of living while the "prince of this world" is still governing, but also the awareness that God can judge his Church and reprove her even through his silence.[3] We must refer to prayers that are not heard, to the disappearance (or quasi-disappearance) of the gift of healing and the other gifts that in great part nourished the life of the first Christian community.

A close look shows that there is a reservation which is neither doubt nor relativization, but rather the understanding that initiative and authority ultimately rest and remain in the hands of God who is free to grant or to withhold his promise. The actualization of the work of Christ is the specific function of the Holy Spirit, and the Holy Spirit is freedom. These brief observations

[3] Cf. Is. 1, 10-17.

enable us to glimpse a basic problematic which seems decisive with respect to the doctrine of the sacraments.

Equally important is the reference to Christ as the first sacrament. If we keep in mind the specifications of K. Barth[4] and E. Schillebeeckx on this point, Christ remains the norm of every sign and every sacrament. Nevertheless, it will be necessary to specify in ecumenical discussion, and not merely within one's own confession, what is the norm and what is the reference to the norm, as well as the subsequent relation between the two. The constant preoccupation of those who carry on the dialogue on the Protestant side is gradually to see the discourse of the Catholic spokesman swing from christology to ecclesiology with the subsequent displacement of the norm from the Lord to the Church.

Christology

I believe that one of the major merits of the book by M. Thurian on the eucharist is that it has reminded us of the dogma of Chalcedon concerning the two natures of Christ. For it may be that the temptation within the heart of Christianity is on the one side to *confuse* Christ with the elements of the supper and on the other to *separate* them, and so repeat—on the plane of the sacrament under examination—the Monophysite and Nestorian heresies.[5]

Confronted with this criterion, Catholics and Protestants will certainly have many questions to consider concerning their differences. M. Thurian himself could be suspected of Monophysite inclinations. In any case, the return to christological dogma seems to us rather stimulating, and we should like to take this occasion to ask the question of Catholic theology as to how it is honored in relation to the doctrine of transubstantiation.

From this point onward, the dialogue is further expanded to include the notion of sacrament in particular and the notion of sign in general.

[4] K. Barth, *Dogmatique* II, 1 (Geneva, 1956), pp. 53-7 (*Die kirchliche Dogmatik* II, 1, Zollikon-Zürich).

[5] M. Thurian, *op. cit.*, pp. 268-9.

Fasting

The Last Supper leads us to take note of the real presence of the Lord in the Church. Hence, it might be useful to reflect on the opposite aspect, that is, on the absence of the Lord and the presence of the tempter expressed in the life of the primitive community through the medium of fasting. The Church of the New Testament indeed knew that she had to reckon with the "prince of this world"; she was aware of the power of temptation and she was conscious that missionaries were sent like sheep in the midst of wolves. Therefore, she accompanied her prayers with fasting, thus manifesting all of humanity's sorrow in the face of the threat of evil.

Now if, on account of our divisions, we presently possess an added motive for imploring God's forgiveness, should we not perhaps take into consideration all that the New Testament tells us about fasting so as to experience together the suffering of our separations through a common and concrete act? Certainly, we possess motives to verify the fact that, behind the difficulties of ecumenical gatherings, forces are operating which are greater than ourselves and mask the presence of him (the devil) who divides man from man and the creature from God.

The presence of the adversary is also a concrete reminder to us that unity is, above all, a victory of God over evil. Our own goodwill and the goodwill of our communities are easily overpowered by this opposition which cannot be governed by man. Fasting in common would seem to be a new way—even though it was known of old—for repeating in an ecumenical fashion: ". . . and lead us not into temptation, but deliver us from evil." [6]

[6] Mt. 6, 13.

Joseph Ratzinger / *Tübingen, W. Germany*

Is the Eucharist a Sacrifice?

The sacrificial character of the eucharist is not a primary question today in the dialogue between Protestant and Catholic theologians. Yet, it does represent one of the crucial differences between these theologies, one of those differences that gave the Reformation its distinctive character, its spiritual and theological cast.

I

LUTHER'S CONCERN

The problem of justification forced Luther to start a new investigation into the true nature of Christian faith; it led him to regard the Catholic outlook on faith as a departure from the authentic essence of this reality. But in regard to the eucharist the problem of justification comes to sharp and tangible focus.

As long as one continues to talk about faith and good works, the import of the question remains vague to the individual Christian. He must live in faith because it is only through faith that he can, indeed must, accomplish God's summons. However, once we focus on the distinctive form of Christian worship, the questions take on immediacy and ready clarity. In Luther's estimation, the Mass—that is, the eucharistic service as a sacrifice

66

—is an abomination, a relapse into pre-Christian, pagan forms of sacrifice. In the eyes of Catholics, the Mass is the Christian way of uniting to worship God, through Christ, in the Church.

In reality, Luther sees the dispute over the Mass as one corollary of the more basic question of justification. In his view the Mass represents a perversion of the authentic nature of Christian faith. Christianity has been subverted at its very core and turned upside down. Here again we see Luther struggling to uncover the ultimate meaning of faith—the question to which his theology returns again and again.

In the last analysis, he sees only two ways to relate to God: by faith or by the law—and these two ways are opposed to one another. When man adopts the law approach, he tries to propitiate God by his own initiative. He offers deeds and good works in order to satisfy God and obtain salvation. In sharp contrast to this approach is the Christ-event, to which the New Testament bears witness. It signifies that God brings an end to all these efforts, which are ineffectual in the last analysis, that God himself, through Christ, gives salvation as a gift, a gift that man can never earn through his own deeds and good works.

Thus the orientation of faith is directly opposed to that of the law. It is the acceptance of God's gracious gift, not the offering of gifts. Christian worship, by its very nature, can only involve receiving, not giving. It is man's thankful acceptance of God's unique salvific action in Jesus Christ, which was performed once and yet satisfies for all time. Thus, the very essence of Christian worship is distorted and completely perverted if the offering of gifts replaces the action of giving thanks. For then the law is replacing grace once again, the sufficiency of Christ's saving action is being denied, and man is trying to save himself by his own efforts and deeds. That is why Luther regards the sacrifice of the Mass as a rejection of grace, as a revolt by man, as a relapse from faith into the law—a relapse so sharply criticized by St. Paul.[1]

[1] We need not make individual references to the extensive writings on Luther. Compare the comprehensive presentation in R. Seeberg, *Lehrbuch*

One cannot help but see the profound theological weight of these considerations, especially since it would be quite easy to set Luther aside and derive similar ideas directly from the New Testament itself. The epistle to the Hebrews, in particular, puts heavy stress on the unrepeatable nature of Christ's priesthood and sacrifice, emphasizing the fact that it happened once for all time, contrasting it with the repetitious sacrifices of the old covenant.

Thus a theology of the sacrifice of the Mass should never pass over these questions lightly. Nothing is accomplished by hiding the problem in a corner and stressing the eucharistic "banquet" exclusively. Burying questions does not further theology's progress, nor does it help the faithful to reach the fullness of life. So what are we to say? It is not easy, of course, to find an answer, and much frank debate will be needed on both sides in order to come closer to it.

I think we can move in the right direction if we realize the fact that Luther's impassioned argumentation is not just negative in tone. It also contains positive points and conclusions. These points might well be summed up under two headings:

1. Christ's salvific activity is the sacrifice that is offered once and satisfies for all time. In it God points up the fruitlessness of our cultic worship by presenting us with the authentic sacrifice of reconciliation. The major theme of the epistle to the Hebrews lies at the heart of Luther's theme.

2. For this reason, Christian worship can no longer consist in

---

der Dogmengeschichte IV/1 (Darmstadt, 1953), pp. 396-407, esp. pp. 405ff.; P. Althaus, Die Theologie Martin Luthers (Gütersloh, 1962). The recent analysis by N. Meyer, Luther und die Messe (Paderborn, 1965), is concerned with the history of liturgical worship. On the present state of Protestant-Catholic differences over the sacrificial character of the eucharist, see P. Meinhold and E. Iserloh, Abendmahl und Opfer (Stuttgart, 1960), and especially the probing study of W. Averbeck, Der Opfercharakter des Abendmahls in der neueren evangelischen Theologie (Paderborn, 1966); on the Catholic side, cf. W. Breuning, "Die Eucharistie in Dogma und Kerygma," in Trierer Theol. Zeitschr. 74 (1965), pp. 129-50; on the Protestant side, cf. G. Voigt, "Christus sacerdos," in Theol. Literat. Zeit. 90 (1965), pp. 482-90, and the fine work of M. Thurian annotated in footnote 9.

offering one's own gifts. Essentially it is our thankful acceptance (*eucharistia*) of Christ's salvific action.

Having said this, we can legitimately assert that Luther's presentation, if properly understood, contains two valid take-off points for developing an authentic Christian concept of sacrifice, and also for understanding the eucharist as a sacrifice in a way that is theologically valid and fully in accord with the New Testament concept of faith.

1. It completely excludes the view that the Mass is a self-sufficient, independent sacrifice. At the same time, however, it raises an urgent question. If the Mass is the offering of Christ's gift to his faithful, must it not involve the presence of this gift in some way, the presence of Christ's salvific activity?

Luther's theology certainly devotes much attention to the personalist orientation of faith—what it does "for me". In fact, it does not look upon God's salvific action as past history. Salvation has meaning and relevance only insofar as it has a relationship to the individual. Luther himself says: "If it is not imparted to me, then as far as I am concerned, it is as if it had not happened. . . . The blood-shedding is real only when it is poured out for me." [2]

This presents us with a new insight. The salvific event, which happened once in history, becomes a present reality for me in the sacramental ceremony. The acceptance of God's gift is not associated with something that is simply past. It is associated with a past event that is being offered here and now.

2. This raises a new line of thought. Thankful acceptance is the Christian type of sacrifice because it signifies the presence of Christ's sacrifice and our fulfillment by him. Melanchthon actually broached these ideas, but his tone was so polemical that Trent found no usable starting point in his work for developing a full-blown treatise on the sacrificial character of the Mass. [3]

---

[2] WA 18, 205; cf. R. Seeberg, *op. cit.*, p. 404; Meinhold-Iserloh, *op. cit.*, p. 53.

[3] "Apologie der Augsburger Konfession, XXIV, 19," in *Die Bekenntnisschriften d. ev.-lutherischen Kirche* (Göttingen, 1952), p. 354. The whole of Article XXIV "On the Mass" deserves consideration in connec-

Here we shall break off our train of thought for the moment and examine the testimony of sacred scripture.

II

New Testament Ideas

Every theology of the Last Supper must start with the words uttered by Christ when he instituted the eucharist. These words are central to any discussion of this topic and have been the subject of countless learned treatises. It seems presumptuous for us to discuss them in a few brief paragraphs and to try to evaluate their significance for our present topic. But here we cannot do a thorough job of exegesis. We shall, as it were, pick up the inquiry at the last stage and extract the central points, insofar as they bear on our present topic.[4]

1. *The Texts*

When we recall these texts, we must start out with the realization that the four accounts of the Last Supper (Mt. 26, 26-29; Mk. 14, 22-25; Lk. 22, 15-20; 1 Cor. 11, 23-26) break up into two groups: the narratives of Matthew and Mark and the accounts of Luke and Paul.

The major differences between these two groups of texts are twofold. First, the Matthew-Mark accounts do not mention a command to repeat the ritual. Secondly, the two groups use different terms for Christ's words over the chalice: Matthew-

---

tion with our questions. The Tridentine rejection of the pure-thanksgiving sacrifice is to be found in Denz. 1753.

[4] Of the extensive bibliography on this question we shall only mention J. Jeremias, *Die Abendmahlsworte Jesu* (Göttingen, 1960); P. Neuenzeit, *Das Herrenmahl* (Munich, 1960); J. Betz, *Die Eucharistie in der Zeit der grieschischen Väter* II/1 (Freiburg, 1961); H. Schürmann, *Der Abendmahlsbericht Lukas 22, 7-38* (Leipzig, 1960[3]: a summary of several larger studies by the same author); F. Leenhardt, *Le sacrament de la Sainte Cène* (Neuchâtel-Paris, 1948); P. Benoit, "Le récit de la cène dans Luc XXII, 15-20," in *Rev. bibl.* 48 (1939).

Mark—"This is my blood of the covenant"; Luke-Paul—"This cup is the new covenant in my blood."

A closer examination of these formulas reveals two further differences of no little importance. In Matthew and Mark, the gift is mentioned specifically as the "blood"; in Luke and Paul, the gift is "the covenant". Furthermore, the former texts refer simply to "the covenant", while the latter speak of the "new covenant".

2. Matthew-Mark: Mosaic Sacrifice

At first glance we seem to be dealing with nothing more than formulary differences. But the deep significance of these differences becomes apparent when we realize that the formulas evoke quite different worlds of Old Testament thought. In other words, the two groups of New Testament texts present two different theologies of the Old Testament. Each formula echoes certain rich strains of Old Testament thought and weaves them into a new and distinctive symphony.

The formula of Matthew and Mark—"blood of the covenant" —is taken from Exodus 24, 8. It calls up the whole covenant theology of Exodus, the cultic concepts and sacrifice-theology of the Pentateuch. The contrast set up between "body" and "blood" in this formulation resumes the Old Testament terminology of sacrifice. The central concept of the Torah—the covenant and its actualization—is subsumed within these words and given a new meaning. In these texts the Last Supper parallels the covenant event at Sinai and the cultic ritual that seals it—the ritual that perdured throughout the history of Israel. And the new Moses, Jesus, contributes the covenant blood of this new covenant-liturgy.

Here we need not dwell on the broad perspectives opened up by this parallel between the Sinai event and the Last Supper: it is played up as the sealing of the covenant, and hence as the establishment of the People of God. But for us the important point is that the notion of "covenant blood" definitely introduces sacrificial overtones into the Last Supper event. The liturgy of

Christ's life and death is presented as a covenant sacrifice which elevates the earlier Mosaic event to a higher plane and endows it with its authentic meaning.

3. *St. Paul: Prophetic Concepts*

When we examine the Old Testament background behind St. Paul's view of the Last Supper, we find ourselves in a different world. While the roots of the accounts of Matthew and Mark are buried in the legal codes of the Pentateuch, the accounts of Luke and Paul hearken back to the theology of the prophets. The reference to a "new covenant" recalls the words of Jeremiah: "Behold, the days are coming, says the Lord, when I will make a new covenant with the house of Israel and the house of Judah, not like the covenant which I made with their fathers. . . . I will put my law within them, and I will write it upon their hearts. . . ." (Jer. 31, 31ff.).

Behind this promise lies the whole covenant theology of the prophets, which stands in sharp contrast to the priestly concepts of the Torah. In the Torah, covenant and cultic worship go together; in the covenant theology of the prophets, cultic worship is subjected to widespread criticism of unprecedented harshness. The self-sufficiency of cultic rituals is challenged outright: "I desire steadfast love and not sacrifice" (Hos. 6, 6; see also 1 Sam. 15, 22; Mt. 9, 13). Living belief in Yahweh and genuine love for one's brethren are depicted as the authentic type of worship; without this, formal external ritual becomes an empty, disgusting farce (see Ps. 40 [39], 7ff.; Ps. 50 [49], 8ff.; Ps. 51 [50], 18f.; Is. 1, 11ff; Jer. 6, 20; 7, 22f.).

The expression "new covenant" evokes this whole strain of Old Testament thought. Fulfillment of God's Word, not empty display, is the hallmark of the new covenant. Standing in sharp contrast to the cultic theology of the Torah, this viewpoint is subsumed into the Last Supper dialogue, and it is cast in a new light. In Luke and Paul, the Last Supper is the culmination of the prophetic viewpoint, just as it was the full realization of the Torah in Mark and Matthew.

In Luke and Paul, the Last Supper represents a victory over cultic ritual and sacrificial practices. It is a victory won by the individual who offers himself instead of rams and bulls: "Sacrifice and offering thou dost not desire, but thou hast given me an open ear" (Ps. 40 [39], 6). Or, as the epistle to the Hebrews reiterates: "Sacrifices and offerings thou hast not desired, but a body hast thou prepared for me" (Heb. 10, 5). In place of sacrificial animals stands the self-offering of Jesus Christ. Criticism of ritual worship has assumed its definitive shape, and the Temple has become superfluous.

4. A Common Ground: The Suffering Servant

Does all this mean that there is a yawning chasm between the two groups of New Testament texts? To answer this question, we must consider another strain of Old Testament theology— one which crops up, in different ways, in both series of texts.

In the texts of Matthew and Mark, Jesus says that his blood is poured out "for many". In the Old Testament, this expression implies a universalist outlook without spatial limits. Luke makes this universalist outlook more concrete, focusing on the cultic community that is actually present "for you". The universalist overtones are not eliminated; they are merely concretized to fit the existential situation.

The expression "for many" evokes the Suffering-Servant Songs of Deutero-Isaiah, and it introduces their key concepts into the Last Supper. The Suffering Servant is said to have borne the sins of many (53, 12), and thus to have made them righteous (53, 11). Moreover, in Isaiah, the concept of the Suffering Servant is linked up closely with the covenant (42, 6; 49, 8). Thus the prophetic concept of the covenant is deepened and enriched. The future covenant is no longer rooted solely in an interiorization of the law, but in the vicarious love of the Servant who suffers on behalf of all. This transforms the core of the prophetic message, and nowhere is it expressed so forcefully as in the Songs of Deutero-Isaiah.

Let us now take another step and try to establish a connection between this strain of Old Testament thought and the conflicting cultic concepts discussed above. We can say this much at least: the image of the Suffering Servant reflects a theology that developed during the Babylonian exile, when Israel had no temple and no cultic worship. During this period it seemed that God had forgotten his people. Cultic worship lapsed, so there was no reason to criticize it. Amid these circumstances Israel glimpsed a new truth: the Israelite nation itself—rejected, destroyed and exiled—is humanity's sacrifice in God's eyes. Its tragic plight represents a sacrifice to God; there is no question of some formal ritual. Israel discovers a new type of sacrifice, one that is much more basic than any which could be offered in the Temple. This new type of sacrifice is martyrdom. Cultic sacrifice is now superseded by man's self-surrender.[5]

H. Schuermann has pointed out that such expressions as "giving up his body" and "giving up his soul" are commonly used in reference to the death of martyrs. Thus "Jesus characterizes his coming death as the death of a martyr".[6] He picks up the Servant of Yahweh notion, interprets his own life and death in this light, and thus confers the definitive meaning on the cultic-worship concept.

Christ depicts himself as the Servant of Yahweh. In him that prophetic image is epitomized and fully actualized. All the theories of cultic sacrifice are now superseded, and the new covenant is sealed and fulfilled by a truly new sacrifice. It becomes apparent that Jesus, the man who sacrifices himself, is the real cultic ritual, the authentic means of worshiping God. All four New Testament accounts bear witness to a new form of worship, which does not consist in ritual acts but in the self-sacrifice of one man who offers himself to the Father for the sake of mankind. The concept of the Servant of Yahweh is the central notion that links them all together and reunites the law and the prophets. We can sum it all up in the words of Johannes Betz: Christ's

---

[5] Cf. J. Ratzinger, "Stellvertretung," in *Handbuch theol. Grundbegriffe,* II, ed. H. Fries (Munich, 1963), pp. 566-75.

[6] H. Schuermann, *op. cit.* (footnote 4), p. 35.

sacrifice "is not to be understood primarily in terms of ritual sacrifice, but in terms of martyrdom; it is a person's total offering of self".[7]

Thus we have come to the heart of the New Testament concept of sacrifice, as it is embedded in the Last Supper accounts. Here the law and the prophets—cultic worship and its critics—achieve their ultimate goal; here they are both "fulfilled". The epistle to the Hebrews picks up this theme once again, weaving a magnificent and thorough theological synthesis. But it does not rely on abstract ideas; it focuses on the reality of Christ's passion.

Christ's life and death exemplifies the authentic aim of Old Testament cultic worship, for all cultic worship is based on the notion of vicarious representation. Human forms of sacrifice are abolished as unworthy in God's eyes. If man wants to let gifts take his place, he must realize that nothing can compensate for him. Sacrificing fruits or animals is not satisfactory; man cannot pay his own ransom (see Mk. 8, 37).

Man cannot sacrifice himself or substitute another sacrifice. The situation seems hopeless. Cultic worship seems to be an exercise in futility. The self-offering of the man Jesus gives full meaning to the notion of cultic worship, and it abolishes previous cultic practices. He himself is the cultic ritual, and it is in this sense that the eucharistic supper is a sacrifice. Through our remembrance of it, it enters our midst.

5. Past, Present and Future

This brings us to the last question: the present-day reality of the eucharistic supper. Here we can only make a few suggestive comments.

This question, too, is brought up in the Last Supper discourse, in Christ's command to "do this in remembrance of me" (Lk. 22, 19; 1 Cor. 11, 24-26). At one time H. Lietzmann believed that these words furnished strong evidence for the Hellenistic origins of the sacramental banquet. He tried to prove that Paul instituted it to draw a parallel with the Hellenistic practice of a memorial

[7] *Ibid.,* p. 40.

meal for the dead.[8] The more recent investigations of J. Jeremias
and M. Thurian have disproved this theory. They show that we
are dealing with a notion rooted deeply in Old Testament theology.[9]

The "memorial" concept is a central notion in the cultic
worship of the Old Testament. It links the Last Supper to the
same thought patterns and traditions that we examined previously. A "memorial" calls something to mind and makes it
actually present. When Israel celebrated her memorial remembrance of salvation history, she embraced it as a present reality;
she stepped within this history and participated in its concrete
reality. It is this notion of "memorial", as well as the fact that
Israel subsumed her cultic worship under this notion, that dis-
tinguishes her cultic ritual from that of her neighbors. The
neighboring cults focused on the cyclic "dying and rising" of the
cosmos; the myth of eternal return took concrete shape in their
rituals.[10] By contrast, Israel's cultic worship is based on God's
dealings with Israel and the patriarchs in history; it brings order
into this history, brings it into mind, and makes it present. It is
in the notion of memorial, of remembrance, that cosmic rituals
and historical faith differ sharply.

There is a further point to be made. The concept of memorial
does not deal solely with the past and the present. It deals, above
all, with the future. It represents man's remembrance of God's
salvific activity and God's recollection of what is yet to come.
It is a summons to put hope and trust in what is to come.[11] The
Pauline account of the institution of the eucharist contains a
remark that points in the same direction: "For as often as you

[8] H. Lietzmann, *Messe und Herrenmahl* (Bonn, 1926), p. 223; compare
his commentary on the first letter to the Corinthians.
[9] J. Jeremias, *op. cit.* (footnote 4), pp. 229-46 (thorough disagreement
with Lietzmann); M. Thurian, *Eucharistie, Einheit am Tisch des Herrn*
(Mainz-Stuttgart, 1963), esp. pp. 15-26 and pp. 125-67: trans. from
Eucharistie (Neuchâtel, 1959); Eng. trans.: *Eucharistic Memorial* (John
Knox, 1961).
[10] Cf. M. Eliade, *The Myth of Eternal Return.*
[11] On the future orientation of the eucharistic "remembrance", see particularly J. Jeremias, *op. cit.*

eat this bread and drink the cup, you proclaim the Lord's death until he comes" (1 Cor. 11, 26).

This "proclaiming" is something more than mere words; it is not purely informational. It is a proclamation of thanks and of hope, which renders something else real and present.[12] It is important to realize this because it brings out the close connection between the spoken word and sacrifice. It points up the important role of "proclamation" in giving reality to the Christian sacrifice as a memorial. It indicates that there is no antithesis between Word and Sacrament, and that we later distorted the nature of both by playing up this notion.

The Fathers of the Church developed the doctrine of the eucharist as a sacrifice on the basis of the scriptural link between Word and Sacrifice. It was a sacrifice realized by the words spoken; the words were stressed more than the sacramental objects.

So we have come full circle. By now it should be evident that the New Testament does not regard thanksgiving and sacrifice as opposites. Rather, each helps to explain and define the other. We have certainly not presented a full-blown dogmatic theory of the eucharist as a sacrifice. But perhaps we have shed some light on the true take-off point for any such theory, and for a meeting of the minds between divided Christians.

[12] Cf. H. Schlier, *Die Zeit der Kirche* (Freiburg, 1958), pp. 249f.; *ibid.*, *Wort Gottes* (Würzburg, 1958), pp. 65ff.; J. Schniewind, "Katangillo," in *Theol. Wörterb. z. N.T.* I, pp. 70f.

Piet Schoonenberg, S.J./*Nijmegen, Netherlands*

TRANSUBSTANTIATION:
How Far Is This Doctrine Historically Determined?

Public interest in the teaching on transubstantiation reached a climax when Pope Paul published his encyclical *Mysterium fidei* on September 3, 1965, just prior to the start of the last session of the Council. This interest had already been shown by a number of publications, mainly, though not exclusively, Dutch. These publications created some commotion here and there as they spread among large sections of the ordinary faithful. In fact, they pursued a theological debate that was already current in many countries. The debate originated in France immediately after World War II; it became general among theologians during the last ten years, and during the last two years began to involve large sections of the people. Moreover, the real presence and transubstantiation were common topics in ecumenical discussions. Therefore, the question is both relevant and actual.

Transubstantiation: The Word and Its Content

In Chapter 4 and Canon 2 of its *Decree on the Eucharist,* the Council of Trent described the change that takes place at the consecration. It then says that this change is called "transubstantiation" by the Catholic Church "conveniently and properly" (*convenienter et proprie:* DS 1642) and "very suitably" (*aptissime:* DS 1652). This was true for the time of that Council, and obviously not for the time when it did not yet exist, and therefore it need not remain so. Even if it was the best term then, other more or less convenient terms may well have existed. Certainly today other terms may be produced which may well be more apt for this age. Whether they are better in fact can only be decided by the present situation and not by an appeal to Trent.

In any case, we are not so much interested here in the term "transubstantiation" as in the underlying doctrine it is meant to convey. What is the meaning of the *conversio* of bread and wine? The Tridentine decree describes it (Ch. 4) as follows: Through the consecration there occurs a change of the whole substance of bread into the substance of the body of Christ our Lord, and of the whole substance of wine into the substance of his blood" (DS 1642). Here the terminal point of this change is called the substance of Christ's body and blood, but in Canon 2 it is simply called his body and blood (DS 1652). The doctrine of transubstantiation refers especially to the substance of bread and wine rather than that of Christ's body and blood. It says specifically that this substance of bread and wine is changed, and this totally (*conversio totius substantiae:* DS 1642, 1652). This implies that the species of bread and wine remain, and the species only (*manentibus dumtaxat speciebus panis et vini:* DS 1652).

Three Interpretations of This Teaching

We have to answer these questions: How far is this teaching on transubstantiation binding for our Catholic belief? To what extent is it subject to historical circumstance and can therefore be superseded? The actuality of the questions demands that we examine what is meant by transubstantiation today. I can suggest three different interpretations that are current.

1. The first one is rather a misinterpretation that is nevertheless very common. The patristic teaching and practice of the eucharist, which must be described as both symbolical and realistic throughout in spite of differences of emphasis, disintegrated in the Carolingian age. From that time on, symbol and

reality were seen as opposed to each other, not only in the liturgy but in the whole cultural situation, and therefore also in the theology of the eucharist. The symbol was understood simply as a pointer, as something that draws attention to something else, as allegory or illustration; the real was what could be seized hold of, what was physical. This view is evident in Amalarius of Metz (9th century) and in the opponents of Berengar (11th century).[1] It flourished in a popular view that fed on stories about bleeding hosts and apparitions in the host.

The great Scholastics countered all this with sharp criticism and developed the teaching of transubstantiation precisely in order to get rid of the contradictions implied in this physical attitude. Accordingly, they put forward a change that did not take place in the physical structure of bread and wine but in their metaphysical reality, although this teaching could find no more room for the old symbolism in its synthesis. The popular attitude, however, persisted even to our own days. What is so tragic is that this attitude is still being justified with the terminology of a transubstantiation doctrine which was elaborated precisely in order to eliminate it. In addition, popular language frequently identifies "substance" with "matter" today. Therefore, it is hardly astonishing that in non-Catholic press reports on *Mysterium fidei* such sentences occurred as: "The pope maintains the material presence of Christ in the eucharist."

2. But even a transubstantiation doctrine that uses the terms correctly can still develop along two lines. It can either take the term "substance" (*substantia*) in a broad and general sense, or it can give it a philosophical and, particularly, an Aristotelian meaning. The former line will oppose "substance" to "outward appearances" (*species*); the latter and stricter view will oppose it to "accidents". As opposed to species, substance means reality, the deepest level of reality, at least when speaking of the eucharist, and then it is opposed to purely outward appearance

---

[1] A. Kolping, "Amalar von Metz und Florus von Lyon," in *Zeitschr. f. Kath. Theol.* 73 (1951), pp. 424-64; P. Engels, "De eucharistieleer van Berengarius van Tours," in *Tijdsch. Theol.* 5 (1965), pp. 363-91.

or purely outward effects. Only this meaning was prevalent in the teaching on the eucharist until it was invaded by the Aristotelian categories. There is nothing that forces us to see more in the term "transubstantiation" that appeared during the second half of the 12th century than in the "substantial conversion" (*substantialiter converti*) and *transubstantiari* as used in a Roman Synod of 1079 (DS 700), or the Lateran Council of 1215 (DS 802), or the Second Council of Lyons in its Confession for the Byzantines of 1274 (DS 860).

However, as Scholasticism, and particularly the teaching of St. Thomas, penetrated into the utterances of the magisterium, the situation changed. The problem then arises whether the councils simply continued to use this general terminology or whether they adopted the Aristotelian meaning and, in their statements, proposed this meaning to our belief.

3. Thus, we reach the third interpretation, linked with the name of Aristotle because it is based on the Aristotelian categories of "substance" and "accident". The word "substance" here refers to the "being" which "underlies" (*sub-stat*) any other feature that is added to it ("lies next to it"—*ad-cidit*), or "accident". Its "accidental" way of being is distinct from that of the "substance". These two terms clearly refer to *what* something is and to *how* it is. All this is part of Aristotle's teaching about "categories". St. Thomas added to this distinction between substance and accident by maintaining that this distinction is *real,* so that substance and accident can even be separated from each other. He was led to this by thinking about the eucharist, and so Schillebeeckx says that Thomas "transubstantiated" Aristotle's thought.[2]

Exactly What Is the Problem?

As regards these questions—How far is the teaching on transubstantiation historically conditioned? How far does it hold for us today?—we may ignore the first interpretation which is a

---

[2] E. Schillebeeckx, "Christus' tegenwoordigheid in de Eucharistie," in *Tijdsch. Theol.* 5 (1965), p. 157.

misconception. The materialistic or physical interpretation may still be widespread, but it is certainly not the official teaching of the Church. Both the second and third interpretations, however, have become part of this teaching and the exact problem therefore is: Which of these two is the real teaching? Did the magisterium pronounce in favor of the Aristotelian interpretation of transubstantiation or in favor of the broader one? This is clearly of great importance; if the broader interpretation is the official one, then such notions as "transfinalization" (transposition of the aim) and "transignification" (transposition of meaning) may mean the same thing as "transubstantiation" (although this does not necessarily imply that the older term has now become superfluous). This would not be possible with the Aristotelian version. In other words, is our eucharistic belief tied up with the Aristotelian "substance-accident" view or is there room for other views? We shall examine this from the viewpoint of four official pronouncements, two from General Councils (Constance and Trent) and two encyclicals (*Humani generis* and *Mysterium fidei*).

The Two Councils of Constance and Trent

Here I shall make use of three articles, of which the second opposes the first and the third tries to reconcile both. Dom G. Ghysen maintains in his *Présence réelle eucharistique et transsubstantiation dans les définitions de l'Eglise catholique*[3] that Trent used the terms "substance" and "species" in a general, broad sense, uninfluenced by any particular philosophy. E. Gutwenger, however, in his *Substanz und Akzidenz in der Eucharistielehre,*[4] holds that the terminology of Constance decided the terminology of Trent and that Constance used "substance" and "accident" in the Aristotelian sense. In *Christus tegenwoordigheid in de Eucharistie,*[5] E. Schillebeeckx agrees with Gutwenger but is firmly convinced that the fathers of Trent were

[3] *Irenikon* 32 (1959), pp. 420-35.
[4] *Zeitschr. f. Kath. Theol.* 83 (1961), pp. 257-306.
[5] *Tijdsch. Theol.* 5 (1965), pp. 136-72 (to be continued).

bound to use the Aristotelian terminology in order to express their belief in the fact and the manner of the real presence at that time, but that we are not bound to express ourselves in that way. Let us look at these three studies.

1. The Council of Constance used the terminology of those whose eucharistic teaching it condemned, namely, John Wycliffe and his followers. Gutwenger shows clearly that in *De Eucharistia tractatus maior* Wycliffe attacked the Aristotelian-Thomist view. Of the forty-five propositions condemned by Constance in 1415, the first three were taken from this work (DS 1151-3). When Pope Martin V confirmed this condemnation in 1418 during the Council (DS 1251), he called Wycliffe's propositions "notoriously heretical", which probably refers to his statements about the eucharist. It would seem obvious, therefore, that both Constance and Wycliffe only thought of Christ's real presence in the sense of the Aristotelian distinction between substance and accident. In order to maintain the belief in the real presence the council had to maintain the distinction against Wycliffe.

2. The same situation obtained in Trent. Both Ghysen and Gutwenger point out that, in its eucharistic teaching, this council remained true to its principle not to interfere in Scholastic disputes within the limits of the faith. But the interpretation of transubstantiation in terms of substance and accident was apparently not seen by the fathers as a Scholastic opinion; they saw it simply as the teaching of Constance. It is true that Trent uses the notions of *substance* and *species,* but in no way does it oppose the interpretation of transubstantiation on the line of substance-accident. Apparently the fathers could not think of it in any other way, although the return to the use of substance-species remains a curious fact. This shows that the statement of belief made by a council or by anybody else can never be satisfactorily detached from contemporary theological thought, and certainly not by those who themselves make that statement.

But we, in a later age, *can* detach the formulation of belief from its historical circumstances. This is brought out particularly by Schillebeeckx, and I wholly agree with him. He points out that the whole discussion of Trent shows that the canon concerning transubstantiation could not possibly have been formulated in any other way if it wanted to affirm the reality of the eucharistic presence. Schillebeeckx emphasizes the point that there was no way open for the fathers to affirm the belief in the eucharistic change of bread and wine, as confessed by the whole tradition, other than by expressing it in terms of the Aristotelian interpretation. Trent, no more than Wycliffe and the fathers of Constance, could see the real presence without the real distinction of substance and accident, although, as Schillebeeckx also observes, it shows a much more sober use of Aristotelian terms and thought. Today, however, this Aristotelian concept, even as developed by the Scholastics, can be criticized without affecting the real presence itself. This possibility must be examined, and here Schillebeeckx asks for a hermeneutical approach to official statements of the Church inasmuch as this approach has already been accepted for the texts of scripture.

The importance of this matter prompts me to make a personal observation. In our Christian belief, we must realize that there are central points that we can in no way deny or accept according to taste. On the other hand, constant thinking about our belief leads us to the discovery that our expression of this belief is inadequate, even in its most central points. This expression of the faith, even of its most central points—whether by the magisterium, the apostles, or even Jesus Christ himself—is always conditioned by the situation that affects every single human statement. Every language, every style, is limited in vocabulary, in grammatical constructions and imagery. Insofar as the magisterium is concerned, its literary genre is the more important since its thought and words must be suited and adapted to questions that are determined by the historical situation. One can never use an earlier statement as a direct reply to questions that were not posed at the time when the statement was made—nor are the presuppositions the same. Among these presuppositions we must count the images and ideas about God and man that are current at a given time, the ideas about the material world, and

therefore, in the age of Scholasticism, the concept of hylo-
morphism, the distinction of soul and body, of substance and
accidents. It has become possible to detach our proclamation of
the Gospel and the Christian view of man from Pythagoras' view
that the earth is the center of the universe. The question now
arises whether we should not dissociate a personal afterlife from
the idea of a soul without a body and the eucharistic presence
from accidents without a substance. We have seen that since
Constance the statements by the magisterium have been influenced by the distinction and separability of substance and accidents, but we saw also that there, and particularly in Trent, the
dominant intention was to affirm and safeguard the belief in the
real presence. Therefore, one should not ask in the case of a
new interpretation of the eucharistic dogma whether it repeats
the words of Constance and Trent, or even whether it develops
the notions that were used there in some direct way, but rather
whether it corresponds to that dominant intention. The use of
other notions and another view of the world, man and God, in
the formulation and solution of the problem, is therefore not a
proof of disloyalty, but rather the only possible loyalty today.

Two Encyclicals

To date, however, the magisterium appears to reject any such
attempts. No doubt, this has been done at a less august level
than that of a council; it has been done in decisions issued by
the Holy Office [now the Congregation for the Doctrine of the
Faith] and more recently in encyclicals. But it would show little
ecclesial spirit if one did not heed these statements. Immediately
connected with the present discussion are the two encyclicals,
Humani generis of Pius XII (1950) and *Mysterium fidei* of
Paul VI (1965).

1. *Humani generis* deals with a number of movements that
are more or less vaguely described, in a pejorative sense, as "new
theology". It refers to some specific assertions, denials or doubts
that characterize this movement. In n. 26 it says the following
about transubstantiation: "You will find men arguing that the

doctrine of transubstantiation ought to be revised, depending as it does on a conception of substance that is now out of date. The real presence of Christ in the holy eucharist is thus reduced to a kind of symbolic communication (*ad quemdam symbolismum reducatur*), the consecrated species being no more than an effectual sign of Christ's spiritual presence and of his close union with his faithful members in the mystical body (*nonnisi signa efficacia sint spiritualis praesentiae Christi:* DS 3891).

In order to judge these words correctly I would like to draw attention to the words that follow in n. 28, immediately after the list of the new notions, a paragraph which has been omitted from DZ. and DS. The pope says that the spread of these and similar opinions forces him "to call attention . . . to falsehoods and approaches to falsehood which are so manifest" (*manifestos errores errorisque pericula . . . indicare*). The assertions are not singly set out in detail so that there is nothing to prevent one from maintaining that the quoted opinion does not belong, according to the encyclical, to the errors but only to opinions that approach error. This claim could be justified because the opinion gives an accurate description of the sacrament in general but makes no mention of the more specific detail.

2. The great conflict about the sign comes out, however, in *Mysterium fidei*. It is probably due to Vatican Council II that this encyclical, in contrast to *Humani generis,* does not fulminate against innovators but rather praises their intention and takes note of their thought and terminology, while nevertheless expressing disapproval and serious warnings (n. 4). The encyclical recalls, first of all, that the eucharist is a mystery, here mainly in the sense of being beyond natural knowledge (nn. 15-22), and that it is necessary to observe the Church's manner of expression (nn. 23-25). Here occurs the curious sentence: "These formulas, like the others which the Church uses to propose the dogmas of faith, express concepts that are not tied to a certain form of human culture, or to a specific phase of scientific progress or to one or other theological school. No, these formulas present that part of reality which necessary and universal experience per-

mits the human mind to grasp and to manifest with apt and exact terms (*aptis certisque vocibus*) taken from either common or polished language" (n. 24). This passage rightly states that the utterances of the magisterium are less closely connected with one or other school of thought than is sometimes suggested, but does it not underrate far too greatly the time and place of such utterances? In the context of the discussion on transubstantiation this passage might imply that, according to the encyclical, the magisterium, and particularly Trent, uses "substance" and "species" only in a very broad sense. This would imply that these two terms stand open to another interpretation than that put forward by Aristotelian Scholasticism.

The other interpretation, labeled at the moment by the terms "transfinalization" and "transignification", is elsewhere rejected by the encyclical as a *"complete explanation"*. Its main thesis, indeed, may be paraphrased as follows: one can point out in the eucharistic change of bread and wine a transfinalization and a transignification (in actual fact, only the latter is referred to here), but only if one adds to these transubstantiation; without this, the interpretation would fall short of the reality of Christ's presence in the eucharist. Yet, it seems to me that the encyclical does not sufficiently distinguish between *two* conceptions of transignification or transference of meaning, and thus between two conceptions of sign and symbol. If one makes this distinction, the intention of the encyclical does not disagree with the present interpretation. This view must be developed by analyzing what the encyclical says about real presence and transubstantiation, and particularly what it rejects as untrue or inadequate.

First, of all, the eucharistic presence must not be conceived as "an omni-presence of the 'pneumatic' nature, to use the current term, of Christ's body in glory" (n. 39). But the main rejection concerns the limitation of the presence to a mere symbolism (*aut illam intra limites symbolismi coarctando:* n. 39), and the encyclical continues to concentrate exclusively on this point. Here the document begins by quoting the passage from *Humani generis* mentioned above. Thus I immediately pass on to the considerations that belong properly to *Mysterium fidei*. To my mind, these seem to reject a particular conception of a change in sign and meaning which is *not* held by those who defend the new interpretation.

When one talks about a "sign", one should use this word, first of all, in the sense of an *action*-sign. A *thing* is in any case only a sign insofar as it is connected with an action-sign. An action, however, can signify in various ways and with various degrees of intensity, and among these there are two that can be clearly distinguished. There are action-signs that *bring something to our knowledge,* and so lead to instruction, provoke feelings or transmit a command (for the latter, think of traffic signals). But there are also action-signs—and here the *action* is of prime importance—where what is shown forth is at the same time communicated or at least offered. The content of this second kind of action-signs is always a kind of love or communion—shaking hands, a kiss, etc. This second kind fully deserves the designation "effective signs", although the first kind is also effective to some degree in that it communicates knowledge and so also establishes some sort of communion, although only very implicitly. We might therefore speak of "informative" signs on the one hand, and "communicating" signs on the other. In spite of a certain overlapping, these two kinds of action-signs are easily distinguished. Even thing-signs can show this difference (compare a traffic light with a gift).[6]

I have distinguished these two sign forms in order to clarify what now follows in the encyclical. From n. 40 on, it develops the following thesis: the eucharist is a symbol (nn. 40-43), *but it is also* truly the body and blood of Christ (n. 44); therefore, the eucharistic change is a transignification, *but also* an ontological transubstantiation. That the eucharist is a symbol is proved by the quotation from the Tridentine *Decree on the Eucharist*

---

[6] Since today the words "sign" and "symbol" are only understood as informative signs, it is necessary in pastoral practice only to use *the word* "sign" after it has been explained as a "communicating sign". A revaluation of the word "communion" may be required here.

which describes it "as a symbol . . . of the unity and the charity with which he wanted all Christians bound and joined together . . . and, thus, the symbol of the single *body* of which he himself *was the head*" (n. 40; DS 1635, 1638). It seems to me that in these texts of Trent "symbol" refers to my second kind of signs, i.e., as effective and communicating. In this way the words echo what the whole of early Scholastic theology expressed by saying that the unity of the faithful or the mystical body of Christ is the fruit, the consequence, the *res* of the "sacrament" of the eucharist. This tradition goes back to St. Paul: "Because there is one loaf, we who are many are one body, for we all partake of the same loaf" (1 Cor. 10, 17). Here the unity comes about through partaking of the one loaf, according to the rule: who eats of the altar becomes a partaker of the altar (v. 18). Here, too, the eucharist is a communicating and effective sign. The encyclical quotes this text in n. 43, while Trent is quoted in n. 40. In between, however, there are two quotations in nn. 41 and 42, from the Didache (9, 1) and from Cyprian (*Ep. ad Magnum* 6), where the eucharist is also seen as a symbol, but differently. Here the kneading of many grains into one loaf and the pressing of many grapes into wine become the symbol of union among Christians. But here the sign is no longer communicating or effective because the milling, kneading, baking and pressing do not bring about the unity of Christians; they are only indicative and figurative signs of this unity.

It is a great pity that nn. 40-43 did not penetrate further into the meaning of the term "symbol" in the quotations. As it stands, the communicating or effective symbol is treated as identical with the merely informative or indicative symbol. And so the conclusion runs: "While the eucharistic symbolism brings us to an understanding (*apte nos ducit ad intelligendum*) of the effect proper to this sacrament, which is the unity of the mystical body, it does not indicate or explain what it is that makes this sacrament different from all others" (n. 44). This is indeed true of the *comparison* between bread and the Church, but to this must be added that "the eucharist is that flesh of our savior" (*ibid.*). If, however, "symbol" is understood as a communicating sign, then this reality is already included, for then the eucharist is the sign in which the Lord gives his body in order to make us into his body and in which he gives himself to us for communion in and with him. To my knowledge this interpretation is the one held by those who, during the last twenty or thirty years, have described the eucharistic change as transignification. That is why they do not have to *add* a real presence to the sign of the eucharist, as the encyclical maintains repeatedly. They have already included this real presence in the eucharist as a communicating and effective sign.

The same applies to what the encyclical says about the way in which the real presence takes place, i.e., about transubstantiation. "As a result of transubstantiation, the species of bread and wine undoubtedly take on a new meaning and a new finality, for they no longer remain ordinary bread and ordinary wine, but become the sign of something sacred, the sign of a spiritual food. However, the reason they take on this new significance and this new finality is simply because they contain a new 'reality' which we may justly term *ontological*" (quam merito *ontologicam* dicimus; italics in the original, n. 46). Here we have again the same procedure: the species undergo a transignification and a transfinalization, *but there is also underneath* a transubstantiation: "Not that there lies under those species (*sub praedictis speciebus*) what was already there before, but something quite different" (*ibid.*). Just as before a *merely informative sign* was declared inadequate for the expression of Christ's presence under the eucharistic species, so here a *merely accidental transignification* is said to be not enough in order to express how this presence comes about. Therefore, a transubstantiation has to be added, and this is then the real thing. But if we consider the finality and the significance themselves as "substantial", as given with the reality of bread and wine and co-constitutive of these elements, then transfinalization and transignification are identical with transubstantiation. Since the encyclical does not mention such a "substantial" transfinalization and transignification, it has not condemned this interpretation. *Nor does it follow from this document that the Aristotelian Scholastic interpretation of transubstantiation is the only one possible.*

My position, then, is that *Mysterium fidei* only denounces as inadequate that symbolism and that change in meaning which exclude a real presence and therefore a real, substantial change of bread and wine. A symbolism and transignification that maintain this realism are not condemned by the encyclical for the simple reason that they have not been mentioned. Even where in a few texts the "sign of Christ's body" is contrasted with "Christ's body itself" (nn. 20, 44, 50), the effective symbol and the ontological, substantial transignification are not rejected. Therefore, the encyclical leaves room for a broader interpretation of transubstantiation that can be elaborated in various ways.

PART II
BIBLIOGRAPHICAL
SURVEY

Wim Luurt Boelens, S.J./*Stadskanaal, Netherlands*

Eucharistic Developments in the Evangelical Church

Religious thought, whether Catholic or Protestant, centers today on the theology of the sacraments and that of the proclamation. We realize more and more that they are closely connected and that there can be no opposition between Word and Sacrament in biblical theology.[1] The interrelation of these two, like their ecclesiological significance and function, is still subject to debate. While there is not yet an official exchange of preachers, Christians of various denominations like to take part in interdenominational services as long as these do not include a celebration of the eucharist. This already shows how great a change is taking place in the whole ecumenical situation. It is based on a mutual reappreciation among the Christian Churches. Even on the Catholic side, several provinces of the Church are encouraging these interdenominational services as leading toward greater Christian unity in thought and practice.[2]

Interest in the sacraments centers mainly on the eucharist, and

[1] H. Schlier, "Die Verkündigung im Gottesdienst der Kirche," in *Die Zeit der Kirche* (Freiburg im Br., ²1958), pp. 244-64.

[2] For Holland: *Bisschoppelijke richtlijnen over grenzen en mogelijkheden van godsdienstige gemeenschap tussen katholieken en protestanten* (Nov. 22, 1961): "That one cannot stop at the minimum of what is desirable is due to the dynamics of ecumenism. There can therefore be progress just as one can observe progress in the interrelations between the Christian Church throughout the world. Much prudence and wisdom are required in guiding this progress" (p. 13).

here most of the attention is given to new ways of celebrating it. But this would hardly be responsible if it were not accompanied by a new theological examination of background and principles. The sacramental celebration is indeed a confession of faith *par excellence,* since this is the most authentic gathering of the believing community.[3]

Theological problems are strongly influenced by the philosophical and theological attitudes of their age, and this holds, too, for the theology of the sacraments. Since modern attitudes differ from those of the Reformation, a different situation has arisen also in the interdenominational debate about the eucharist. This change is largely due to a new biblical theology. It is also influenced by a new situation that has brought the Churches into closer sociological and theological contact with each other than ever before. All these factors have broken the deadlock between the Reformation and the Counter-Reformation and have opened up fresh possibilities between the various movements of the Reformation as well as between Rome and the Reformation. We want to examine this new situation here in content and perspective.

1. *Toward a Consensus about the Last Supper within Protestantism*

The Evangelical Church of Germany (EKD)[4] organized six conferences of prominent Lutheran and Calvinist theologians and exegetes between 1947 and 1957 which led to the Theses of Arnoldshain.[5] The many reactions, for or against, to this study

[3] L. Villette, *Foi et sacrement.* Travaux de l'Institut Catholique de Paris, 5 (Paris, 1959).

[4] For the Protestant situation in Germany, see H. Brunotte, *Die Evangelische Kirche in Deutschland* (Hanover, 1959). The EKD is a federation of 28 State Churches (*Landeskirchen*), of which 13 are Lutheran, 2 Reformed and 12 United (with a combination of Lutheran and Reformed Confessional documents).

[5] W. Boelens, *Die Arnoldshainer Abendmahlsthesen.* Van Gorcum's Theologische Bibliotheek, 37 (Assen, 1964). The text of the eight Theses appears on pp. 50-6, and an extensive bibliography on pp. 369-86. The most prominent members of the Commission were G. Bornkamm, J.

project made it an important factor in the shaping of contemporary thought about the eucharist. The course of the discussions, several papers of which have been published, proved of international and interdenominational importance. It was important, for example, for the "Consensus about the Last Supper" between the Reformed and the Lutheran Churches of Holland in 1956.[6]

The "Theses" are also likely to be of practical importance for German Protestantism, inasmuch as a new commission, composed of representatives of various State Churches (*Landeskirchen*), stated in January, 1966, that the members of a State Church of the EKD could also partake of the Last Supper in a church with a different Confession.[7]

One of the most valuable experiences of the conferences which led to the Theses of Arnoldshain was that the discussion ran aground whenever it started from traditional teaching and terminology. To get out of this impasse, it was necessary to go back to the essence of the biblical message with the help of modern exegesis. At the beginning, this return to the sources did not lead to a solution but rather to wide discrepancies. Finally, agreement was reached on the essence of the Last Supper, although this meant that a number of traditional and not always unimportant distinctions had to be set aside. This was thought to be allowable because various biblical data seemed to suggest a greater variety than would have been allowed in earlier days, though it did not endanger the unity of the Church. Seen from this angle these discussions within Protestantism are also important for our own changing position in the ecumenical situation.

Jeremias, E. Käsemann, K. G. Kuhn, E. Michel, A. Oepke, E. Schweitzer, E. Bizer, W. van Loewenich, E. Wolf, E. Sommerlath, W. Kreck, H. Gollwitzer, P. Brunner, H. Iwans, H. Vogel, E. Schlink, F. Deelekat, H. Meyer and W. Niesel.

[6] C. Mönnich and G. van Niftrik, *Hervormd-Luthers Gesprek over het Avondmaal* (Nijkerk, 1958).

[7] The proposal to change Article 4, 4 of the Grundordnung of the EKD can be found in *Luth. Monatsch.* 5 (1966), pp. 204-6. A report on this second Last Supper Commission occurs on pp. 243-6. The relevant papers had not yet been published when this article was written.

2. Divergences in the Interpretation of Luther

In order to understand the differences within Protestantism about the Last Supper, we must remember that it is not merely a matter of Lutheranism versus Calvinism. There are equally sharp contrasts within Lutheranism that also appear in the interpretation of the Last Supper. On the whole, one may say that there is opposition between the interpretation based on the early Luther (1518-25) and that based on the later one (1525-45).[8]

The theology of the early Luther was characterized by criticism of a Catholicism that had become a matter of outward appearances. This caused him to put the function of personal faith and a correspondingly powerful preaching of the Gospel at the heart of his theological thinking. In the words of the institution of the Last Supper, Luther seemed to have ears only for the message: Christ's blood has been shed for you. Here one hears the overtones of his teaching on justification. The effect of the eucharistic celebration lies in the growth of the sense of community and in the experience of being redeemed in faith. He took the real presence, as it were, for granted. During this period this fact of faith was seen rather as an aid to belief in the redemption against all opposition. He explicitly rejected the subtle Scholastic distinctions used to make the real presence intelligible in human terms, and this implies such points as concomitance and transubstantiation. The believer's subjective acceptance of forgiveness and trust in God is more prominent than what happens objectively in the sacrament.[9] The words of the institution are seen more as a message of redemption for man's existence than as consecrating words for the elements of bread and wine.[10]

The gift of Christ's body and blood is seen as the seal affixed to the new covenant. It is a confirmation of the proclamation and

[8] The positions of the more important representatives have been compared with Luther by W. Boelens, *op. cit.*, pp. 118-253. The left wing, which bases itself on the early Luther, is strongly influenced by Bultmann. The right wing (or Confessional Lutheranism) is mainly represented by those Lutheran Churches that are associated with the VELKD.

[9] *WA* 10, III, 48, 31-49.

[10] *WA* 6, 357, 10-12 and 18.

therefore has but a secondary function: to strengthen the faith.

In all this it is clear that Luther and Calvin have much in common, although they differ on the instrumentality of the bread and wine. Calvin was more cautious with regard to the sacramental signs as a guarantee of salvation.[11] With Calvin, Luther can say that the kerygmatic message of the words of institution is more important than what Luther calls "the sacrament".[12] But further on Luther can defend, as equally obvious, the identity of bread and body: the bread IS the body of the Lord. And then he explicitly rejects the exclusively symbolic interpretation that the bread SIGNIFIES the body of the Lord.[13] In doing so he keeps on referring with his simple obstinacy to the literal interpretation of the words of the institution. But he also denies that the eating of Christ's body means exclusively the incorporation into the mystical body of the Church.[14]

In controversy with the upholders of a purely spiritual interpretation such as Karlstadt, Oecolampadius and Zwingli, Luther abandoned his simple and direct proclamation of salvation. In order to defend his sacramental realism he began to use the Scholastic distinctions and terminology of his age, which occasionally exceeded the limits of sound theology.[15]

Since Luther's later attitude was hampered by the one-sided approach of his opponents, he had great difficulty in achieving a balanced view of the relation between proclamation and sacraments. But it remained typical of him, in contrast with later Calvinistic theology, that he always linked the special saving presence of the Lord closely to the celebration of the eucharist with bread and wine. Here the whole economy of salvation is seen in the sacramental light of an incarnational interpretation of Christ and the Church.[16] This is particularly evident in his main writings about the Last Supper. Even when in later years he was forced

[11] *WA* 6, 230, 23-5.
[12] *WA* 11, I, 432, 21-30.
[13] *WA* 11, I, 434, 5-16.
[14] *WA* 11, I, 437, 14-20.
[15] *WA* 26, 442, 39—443, 2.
[16] *WA* 18, 181, 19-22.

to use precise notions and distinctions which created a "thing-like" and static impression, he remained essentially personalist and dynamic in his thinking about the faith. This point is very important for a consensus about the Last Supper. Somehow or other Luther dealt with every aspect of the Last Supper. But this usually happened in controversy, and so the treatment is one-sided and rarely comprehensive. His teaching was never generally accepted by the Reformation. Just as Luther drew a sharp distinction between himself and his opponents, so Lutheran orthodoxy appealed in its controversy with Calvin and the later Calvinists to the sacramental terminology of the later Luther, and this hardened the differences.

But even within present-day Lutheranism there is a deep rift between those who appeal to the "original reformation" of the younger Luther and those who want to include his later development. The former, with their allegiance to the younger Luther who developed his theology in controversy with Rome, usually have some difficulty with the Catholic approach to the sacraments. Among them one can range the representatives of the so-called kerygmatic theology, among whom the followers of Rudolf Bultmann are outstanding in all their variety.[17] For their existentialist exegesis and interpretation of human life, they appeal to Luther's teaching on justification, which was given its most pungent expression in the early period. This does not leave much room for the objective realities of sacrament, function and institution in the Church. In contrast, there is confessional Lutheranism, particularly the "high-Church" movement, which feels strongly about the confessional writings and takes the function, liturgy and the formation of the community very seriously. This view is based on an exegesis and a biblical and systematic theology with a certain bias.[18]

---

[17] E.g., G. Ebeling, E. Fuchs and E. Käsemann.

[18] Strict Confessional Lutherans are represented by H. Sasse, E. Sommerlath, and the Evangelical Lutheran Synodical Conference; the broader tendency by P. Brunner, P. Meinhold, E. Kinder, and a large section of the Evangelische Michaelsbruderschaft and the Lutheran Churches associated with the VELKD. E. Schlink and P. Althaus stand for the via

These two diverging tendencies of Luther's thought have far-reaching consequences for both preaching and practice and explain the resistance of the tradition-bound communities to the "progressives". Yet, an outright rejection of kerygmatic theology would not do justice to the genuine Christian values contained in it. This is evident from the fact that this theology has given rise to tendencies that led to a rediscovery of the Christian mission to the world. So it initiated a "secular theology" in a movement which paradoxically clings to Luther's teaching on justification with its rejection of "good works". These paradoxes came to the fore in the discussions at Arnoldshain.

3. The Position of Calvinistic Christianity

It is difficult to relate Calvinism to the complicated situation of Lutheranism, and the more so since contemporary Calvinism itself shows several diverging tendencies. In any case, it is impossible to oppose Lutheranism as such to Calvinism as such, although each has its own mentality. Thus, the Calvinist-tinted theology of Karl Barth which paid more and more attention to Church, function and sacrament, exercised a powerful influence on certain sectors of "confessional" Lutheranism. This is obviously the case in the United State Churches (*Unierte Landeskirchen*) which accept both Lutheran and Calvinistic confessional documents. Where Lutherans opposed Bultmann and his followers, they found in Barth a welcome supporter.

Contemporary Calvinism also contains small but important "high-Church" groups, as manifested by the periodical *Verbum Caro* and the Community of Taizé. In their interest in function, sacrament and liturgy they do not yield to "high-Church" Lutheranism.[19] All this means that for the present inter-Protestant dis-

---

media. A similar situation obtains in Scandinavia. In Sweden the high-Church wing is centered on Upsala, the left wing on Lund. This complex situation is important but at the same time difficult for Lutheran research today. An important collection of official Lutheran positions with regard to the Last Supper in Europe and North America has been published in *Kirche und Abendmahl,* ed. V. Vajta (Berlin, 1963).

[19] Typical writings on this eucharistic doctrine are M. Thurian, *L'Eucharistie, Mémorial du Seigneur, Sacrifice d'action de grâce et d'inter-*

cussion about the Last Supper, the situation has become very different from what obtained at the beginning of the Reformation when Lutherans and Calvinists faced each other over a carefully laid down boundary. The question is whether a consensus on the Last Supper stands a better chance now than formerly. The return to the sources of Christianity *via* modern exegesis is important here, as the discussions of Arnoldshain have shown.

4. *Ecumenical Possibilities Created by the New Biblical Approach*

In the critical questions about the right faith of their opponents in the controversy about the Last Supper, the Protestants concentrated with fatal exclusiveness on a highly detailed theological formulation of the structure of the real presence rather than on its function. Here Zwingli clearly rejected the Lutheran interpretations of the identity of the elements with the body and blood of Christ, the oral consumption, the consumption by the "impious" and the local presence. Calvin and his followers opted for the term of "real presence", but defined the presence of the Lord as being "in the power of the Holy Spirit" because the Lord was present bodily only in heaven. This *articulum extra Calvinisticum* became for Lutherans and Catholics the paramount reason for rejecting the Calvinistic interpretation as too "spiritual". Any discussion starting from this static and historically determined terminology seems bound to be futile, since it does not fit in with the essence of the biblical message or with contemporary religious thought. In any case, it is clear that this formulation of the problems can only be considered after closer theological examination. Thus, one understands why the theologians of Arnoldshain, in their courageous attempt to achieve intercommunion *via* a consensus, looked for a biblical teaching about the eucharist in the data provided by contemporary exegesis. The effects of the study of *Formgeschichte,* which cast a remarkable light on

---

cession (Neuchâtel-Paris, 1959); R. Boon, *Offer, Priesterschap en Reformatie* (Nijkerk, 1966) and J. Plooij, *De mysterie-leer van Odo Casel* (Zwolle, 1964),

how the original Christian communities and their hagiographers elaborated Jesus' message theologically, made several Protestant exegetes skeptical about the possibility of ever getting to know the original context, form and intent of Jesus' institution.[20] Thus, it is for many an open question whether the framework of the Last Supper was really a Jewish passover meal. Starting from the Jews' dynamic concept of salvation, which we must presuppose in Jesus, they also reject the static predication of IS. They think, rather, that Jesus spoke in parable form. On the other hand, the same exegetes underrate the fact that the evangelists who think and write in Greek emphasized the Lord's saving presence in what happens officially and ecclesially at the eucharist. Moreover, the way in which the institution narratives were edited was largely determined by the liturgical texts of the communities with which the authors were connected.[21] No doubt, the various authors put a different emphasis on the instrumentality of bread and wine, but all consider it important. Apart from the features they have in common, individual authors stress particular aspects of the eucharist in their own way. Thus, Paul and Luke stress the eschatological aspect, while Matthew and Mark stress the idea of sacrifice.

Some exegetes take an exaggerated pleasure in discovery and try to radicalize these differences of emphasis into contradictions.[22] They will not attach much importance to a doctrinal consensus in our ecclesial situation with an appeal to antiquity. But even those exegetes who champion a comprehensive view on good grounds must admit that the present state of biblical theology cannot justify the traditional appeal to biblical texts in order to maintain the opposition of the early Reformation in its simple form. Both Lutherans and Roman Catholics begin to see that the *praedicatio identica* does not throw much light on the real pres-

---

[20] There is an excellent and balanced study by J. Jeremias, *Die Abendmahlsworte Jesu* (Göttingen, ³1960).

[21] H. Schürmann, *Der Abendmahlsbericht Lucas 22, 7-38* (Paderborn, 1963).

[22] W. Marxsen, *Das Abendmahl als christologisches Problem* (Gütersloh, ²1965).

ence if we want to get to the essence of the sacrament (*proprium sacramenti*). The Last Supper will have to be interpreted in the light of its organic place in the ecclesiological context where the presence of the Lord of the Church is permanently active in the proclamation and the interrelationship of the believers.

Among Calvinist theologians there is now a feeling that the saving instrumentality of earthly gifts and structures was more strongly emphasized in the early Church than Calvinist orthodoxy liked to believe, and that this did in no way compete with the pneumatology of the early Christians. Even more important, they see that, according to the data of the bible, sacramental liturgy was more important than is the case in most Calvinist Churches today. Theological reflection, adjusted to this biblical approach, opens up new possibilities for the dialogue between Lutheran and Calvinist Churches, although centuries of separate development still make them think and feel in a different climate. A consensus about the Last Supper will not lead here to uniformity; this is not the intention, as has been emphasized repeatedly.[23] Biblical reorientation has brought about a change of perspective that allows for a difference in religious practice today as long as this difference does not lead to a radical hardening of positions.

5. *Agreement in Essentials*

In order to restore the celebration of the Last Supper to its central position within the life of the Church, a confession of its institution by Jesus Christ in the sense of worship is required. To imbue the eucharist with a special value as sign and saving power inevitably needs a special act of institution by the God-Man, as the New Testament clearly suggests. If this institution or inauguration is attributed to the creative inventiveness of the early Christians, one may easily be inclined to limit its sign value to a noetic symbol. In that case the old dilemma of a choice be-

---

[23] Articles 8 and 9 of the Dutch Consensus about the Last Supper. The Foreword to the Theses of Arnoldshain admits that the Commission dropped some important traditional points; cf. W. Boelens, *op. cit.*, p. 50.

tween *significat* and *est* is bound to lurk in the background, if
not mentioned explicitly. There are sectors in the Calvinist tradition, and even more in the Lutheran tradition, where much
attention is paid to the liturgical practice of sacramental worship.
However, these will encounter some difficulty since sacrament and
liturgy only occupy a secondary place for great numbers of
Protestants. This is apparent, for instance, when one sees how
little feeling there is among modern Protestant exegetes for an
examination of the rich Old Testament data about the sense of
cult at the celebration of the passover and its use in the interpretation of the Last Supper. This was one of the reasons why
at Arnoldshain the theme of representation and sacrifice was not
even mentioned, as if these thoughts could be alien to Jesus the
Jew.[24] It is important for the whole Christian community that
the Reformers saw the sacrament in the perspective of the proclamation of salvation, and so could underline the personalist and
dynamic aspect of the sacramental celebration. In the search for
a consensus about the Last Supper, it is already a gain if one
can confess the sacramental celebration as the climax of the
proclamation and communication of salvation, which is already
happening in many places. For a genuine and well-founded intercommunion, other aspects will have to be introduced in order to
determine the essence of the sacrament.

In the present discussion much thought is given to the *eschatological* and *ecclesiological* aspects of the eucharistic celebration.[25]
In conjunction, these two aspects show an important improvement on the position of the old Reformers. As Lord of the
Church, Christ acts through his community and invites his followers to the supper table. Thus he molds his Church in a special
way so that during this celebration the Church is already shown
forth as the final, eschatological community of salvation.[26]

The pursuit of this datum of faith is very important ecumen-

[24] H. Gollwitzer agreed with this in a review of my study in *Luth.
Rundschau* 16 (1966), pp. 128-35.

[25] *Die Arnoldshainer Thesen* 1, 2; 3, 4; 6, 3; *Nederlandse Consensus
over het Avondmaal*, Art. 6.

[26] *Arnoldshainer These* 6, 2.

ically because it steers away from the old Reformers' preoccupation with the invisible Church of the true faithful. It also brings
out the distinction between the service of the Word and Sacrament in the strict sense. The proclamation of the Gospel is addressed to both believers and unbelievers, the sanctified and the
sinners. The proclaimed Word of God creates the faith in him
who hears it in grace, but does so as a challenge and an invitation. It does not show visibly and in the concrete whether the
preaching has reached its aim or whether the hearer has accepted
the proffered salvation with his whole being. The ecclesial boundaries of salvation remain to a certain extent vague and invisible
in the case of preaching.

On the other hand, those who answer the invitation to the
eucharist signify in a concrete way that they accept the proclamation with all its consequences, both vertically and horizontally,
i.e., as contact with God through the instrumental salvation of
the Church. At the sacramental celebration of the eucharist the
force and meaning of the proclamation are expressed and fulfilled in the most noble and concrete manner. Thus, those who
approach the communion table show forth the eschatological
community of the People of God.

The Reformed Churches are aware of the consequences that
flow from this ecclesiological and eschatological interpretation.
They see that this runs counter to an attitude that avoided the
eucharist, based, from the Calvinist point of view, on an over-
emphasis on predestination, which has been considerably toned
down in recent times. If more stress is put on the Lord's invitation
than on one's own judgment of the truth, the Reformation may
experience a more intensive practice of this sacrament. This is
expressed in the last Thesis of Arnoldshain: "Since the Lord is
rich for all that call on him, all members of his community are
invited to the Lord's supper. And all that long for God's right-
eousness are promised forgiveness of sins." [27]

As a third advance on the position of the old Reformers we
must mention the *pneumatology* of contemporary Protestant the-

[27] *These* 8, 3.

ology. While the Lutherans confessed the presence of the Lord in the eucharist, the Calvinists believed in the abstruse *extra Calvinisticum* (Christ's humanity is only present in heaven) and, along with this, in a presence of the Lord "in the Holy Spirit". In reply, Lutheran theologians have stressed that Luther did not consider the eucharist as brought about in an exclusively "christological" manner, while attributing the application of the fruits of the eucharist to the operation of the Holy Spirit. It is too often forgotten that, at the heart of Luther's thought, there is the fact that we are brought into contact with the historical event of salvation through the working of the Spirit in Word and Sacrament. His whole vision of the existential acceptance of salvation is based on this fact. But Luther stresses that the Spirit works in the service of Christ; his pneumatology serves his christology and corresponds to it.[28]

On the other hand, Calvinist theologians begin to admit that setting up what may be called an anti-incarnational theology in order to safeguard God's freedom and omnipotence shows a biased and unbiblical theology.[29] This would exclude any guarantee of salvation in the Church or in the Church's official sacramental actions, and the Spirit would become a doubtful element. A Calvinist rightly criticizes the Roman Catholic consecration for not having an epiclesis because this leaves out an essential part of the sacramental action. They are not satisfied, and justifiably so, with the meager reply that this omission—equally unacceptable to the Eastern Orthodox—does not render the consecration "invalid". The Calvinist theologians seem, however, characteristically to stress the pneumatological epiclesis in order to draw attention away from the consecration of the elements. But this brings us back to what all mean to confess—namely, that a presence of the Lord, which is objective but not accepted by man, cannot be basically a saving presence of the Lord. How-

---

[28] A. Peters, *Realpräsenz, Luthers Zeugnis von Christi Gegenwart im Abendmahl.* Arb. zur Gesch. und Theol. des Luthertums, 5 (Berlin, 1960), pp. 46-67.

[29] G. van Niftrik, *op. cit.,* pp. 138-58, where Prof. A. van Huler is criticized.

ever, the Lutheran's realism allows him to confess the Lord as judge in a more concrete manner in this sacramental emergency. The less we have to presuppose a pneumatological opposition in the Calvinists, the more there is a chance of achieving a consensus. Nevertheless, in spite of the differences in mentality, the positions are closer than they were at the time of the Reformation.

The most important advance, however, in the contemporary debate is that the traditional test—what is the function of bread and wine at the eucharistic celebration?—is now admitted to allow of an answer only in the wider framework of a sacramental theology, and so has been reduced to a secondary place. A similar process seems to be taking place among Catholics as well, so that this may open up a broad ecumenical discussion in which the Catholic Church can also take part. A genuine Protestant theologian like Helmuth Gollwitzer, who contributed so much to the formulation of the Theses of Arnoldshain, gave it as his opinion that these Theses would have gained considerably in depth if present-day Catholic theology had been taken more seriously into account. For centuries it appeared—and many faithful are still convinced—that a particular realistic theology about the *manner* of the real presence was sufficient as a test of orthodoxy of faith in the matter of the eucharist. However, it is quite possible that such a theology has left out so many aspects of the sacrament that it is extremely meager as a theology of the eucharist. This has often been marked by insufficient distinction between the essential faith or dogma and theological speculation, although the Church has always allowed this speculation a generous measure of freedom.

It is therefore possible in our age to reach a consensus about the eucharist that may satisfy many parties. This may say less about the *manner* of the real presence but more about other aspects that are better founded in New Testament exegesis and were more fully appreciated in the early Church. If these aspects of incarnation, ecclesiology and pneumatology are taken seriously, the saving activity of the Lord will stand out more clearly and lead to a better understanding of the real presence.

This consideration prompts us to be cautious when we examine theological speculation about the real presence and the functions of bread and wine at the Last Supper. Although we are not happy with the complicated and somewhat obscure formulation of the fourth Thesis, which deals with this, we must admit that the essence of the eucharistic faith is expressed when it is held that the communicant receives the Lord with bread and wine in the sense that they are given in the liturgical celebration. Bread and wine, which before had a purely physical and biological function, then receive essentially a function toward redemption and sanctification in the faith. They are given a totally different intent and significance that modern Catholic theology describes with the words "transfinalization" and "transignification". If the Lord, by virtue of his creative power, identifies himself with the elements of bread and wine and so gives himself with the gifts of bread and wine, then bread and wine are no longer the same as before. Functionally they are lifted above themselves so that at the reception the whole attention is directed to the Lord who gives himself in view of working his redemption.

This tentative Catholic thinking about the eucharist runs parallel with the Protestant attempt to achieve a doctrinal consensus. Both share the personalistic and dynamic tendency that is rather different from the former static theology. If there is room for freedom in Catholic thought, the same freedom must be allowed on the Protestant side. This has its consequences for a dialogue between Protestant Churches and the Catholic Churches of East and West. There are, however, likely to be difficulties in connection with the ecclesiological structures.

6. Ecclesiological Approaches

The theological debate about the eucharist among the Protestant Churches aims at bringing about intercommunion. Agreement about eucharistic doctrine is for many, such as the VELKD (The United Evangelical Lutheran Church of Germany), not enough to proceed to intercommunion because there are other important differences of belief. According to the early Church and the Reformation, the eucharist is meant to be the sign and reflection of an ecclesial community that demands not only communion in baptism and eucharist but also in proclamation. Inter-communion, open or limited, will depend on the Confession and confessional documents that are considered binding. The Con-ference of Faith and Order of Lund (1952) drafted a useful list of the possibilities.[30]

But even if in the search for Church unity one begins with a discussion about the eucharist, one can see that this will touch on all aspects of the faith, for the celebration of the eucharist is the heart and climax of the Church's life of faith. This implies christology, ecclesiology, pneumatology and the official structure. When there is unity on all these points, the eucharistic celebra-tion is indeed the sign of a genuine Church unity. A celebration without unity of faith would give the lie to the eucharistic sign.

For the People of God on pilgrimage and still looking for unity, the eucharist may also be instrumental in bringing about more fully that unity which is already there in principle. We can never presuppose a perfect unity at the eucharist. There is always the tension between the "is" and the "ought to be". But then the Protestant Churches, in their segmented situation, ask the very practical question: How far must the Church's unity be presup-posed and established before one can proceed to intercommun-ion? The answer to this question depends a great deal on how one judges the function of the eucharist insofar as it shows what is present and what ought to be.

The present situation is no longer polemical, as at the Ref-ormation, but ecumenical. Today the search for and the estab-lishment of Christian unity stand in the foreground. In spite of all our differences we recognize our unity in Christ.[31]

Prominent Protestant theologians stress that there is no need

---

[30] Evang. Kirchenlexicon I (2nd ed., Göttingen), "Abendmahlsgemein-schaft," col. 29: (1) Full communion: between Churches of the same Confession; (2) Intercommunion, including intercelebration: reciprocal admission by official consent; (3) Intercommunion without intercelebra-tion; (4) Open communion: admission of any guests that are present; (5) Mutual open communion, including permission for members to receive communion elsewhere; (6) Limited open communion: admission of guests in emergency cases; (7) Closed communion.

[31] A. Nygren, Christus und seine Kirche (Göttingen, 1956).

to bring about the organizational expression of this already-given unity before we can partake of the same supper of the Lord. Thus, the Swedish Lutheran Church is satisfied with minimal demands for a doctrinal agreement to allow many others to her communion, even Baptists and Methodists. They practice intercommunion with the Anglicans. In Holland the Reformed and Lutheran Churches practice open communion since the Consensus about the Last Supper (1956), where, contrary to the Theses of Arnoldshain, the doctrinal differences are frankly admitted.

In Germany, open communion has been the practice for a long time, although not officially supported. In fact, it has become impossible to apply discipline, since the confessional boundaries no longer coincide with the territorial ones. To this one should add the uncontrollable situation of the massive communities of the great towns. It is to the credit of the Evangelical Church of Germany that she did not limit herself to this limited open communion, forced upon her by circumstances, but rather took the difficult path of trying to reach intercommunion *via* the discussion about eucharistic doctrine. This has not yet been achieved. The Theses of Arnoldshain are in fact a study project commissioned by the federation of German State Churches (EKD). A second commission, composed of representatives of the Lutheran, Calvinist and United State Churches, discussed, between 1963 and 1965, whether the plan of Arnoldshain could justify intercommunion and to what extent. The commission seems to have thought that one could proceed to intercommunion without intercelebration. If this is accepted as valid, every State Church will have to conform. To achieve this the authorities of every Church have been presented with a new text for Article 4, 4 in the *Grundordnung* (the basic order) of the EKD: "In all Churches that are associated with the Evangelical Church of Germany, participation in the eucharist, which they celebrate in faithfulness to their Confession, is open to all, and also for those members who hold another Confession which is valid within the Evangelical Church of Germany. This does not affect the juridical Church member-

ship or the juridical regulations of each Church concerning ec-
cclesiastical discipline." [32]

Hopefully, the difficult path followed by the EKD in order to
arrive with great risks at a theologically justified intercommunion
will not frighten other Churches away from similar efforts. The
changed situation of the Churches presupposes another "Church
unity" as the condition for intercommunion than was the case in
the old Church. Caution in the use of intercommunion insofar
as it leads to full communion will stimulate the Churches to keep
on striving after full ecclesiastical communion according to the
Spirit of Christ. This does not exclude pluriformity, as is shown
by early Christianity, even in eucharistic doctrine. But it cannot
be a pluriformity of positions that are radically opposed to each
other.

The Protestant experiment with intercommunion also contains
a challenge for the Catholic Church. Among Roman Catholics
we have only begun to think about an imperfect communion in
connection with an imperfect, yet real, unity of faith. Here, too,
there are desires and initial experiments that will force clergy
and theologians to think seriously about a new approach, which
they cannot brush aside with a simple appeal to the past. The
Decree on the Catholic Churches of the Eastern Rite allows intercommunion between Roman Catholics and Eastern Catholics.[33]
This may have consequences for theology and for religious practice. Here an imperfect sacramental unity, always considered valid
for baptism, is accepted as the expression of an imperfect yet genuine union and recognition. If Protestant communities are recognized as "Church", in whatever form—and Vatican Council II
definitely pointed in that direction—could this not lead to a perhaps very occasional and imperfect "limited open communion"?

Catholics, particularly, should study the ecumenical implica-
tions of sacramental theology.

---

[32] *Luth. Monatsch.* 5 (1966), p. 205.

[33] F. van Beek made an important contribution to this new way of
formulating the problem in "Proeve van een ecumenische beschouwing
over de sacramenten," in *Bijdragen* 26 (1965), pp. 129-79; Eng. tr.: "To-
wards an Ecumenical Understanding of the Sacraments," in *Journal of
Ecumenical Studies* 3 (1966), pp. 57-112.

Olivier Rousseau, O.S.B./*Chevetogne, Belgium*

Divorce and Remarriage: East and West

In a preface to the work of Dauviller and De Clercq, *Le mariage en Droit canonique oriental,* G. Le Bras wrote: "Historians of Canon Law, who have for some time been seeking to expand their discipline, dare to hope that the establishment of a course on the law of the Eastern Churches will provide the first answer to their desires in the major universities." [1] Then, no doubt without realizing that such a proposal might one day reveal differences between two mentalities which stem from the same Christian roots, he cited in support of his desire the favorable vote on this project obtained in 1930 by the jurist R. Généstal of the Ecole des Hautes Etudes at the Sorbonne.

On September 29, 1965, a highly unexpected intervention on the part of the Melkite patriarchal vicar of Cairo, Elie Zoghby, took place in the *aula* with the precise suggestion to expand the present discipline of the Catholic Church concerning marriage along the lines of the Eastern discipline; for the Council was—in the mind of Pope John XXIII—a time of mercy and not condemnation. This intervention was received in different ways, but never in the sense desired by Le Bras.[2] Offered as an inter-

[1] J. Dauviller and C. De Clercq, *Le mariage en Droit canonique oriental* (Paris, 1936), pp. x-xi.

[2] A. Wenger, who devotes a number of pages to this affair in his book *Vatican II, IVe session* (Paris, 1966), cites a letter of J. Dauviller com-

pretation on Matthew 19, 9: "Whoever puts away his wife, except for immorality (*porneia*), and marries another, commits adultery", it has raised a problem periodically posed in theology, even if only on the speculative plane: "Is it permissible to use the Matthean clause to tolerate not only the separation of spouses but also the remarriage of the innocent partner in case of infidelity?" [3]

In more recent times, exegetes have grappled with the Matthean text and reshaped it in every sense,[4] but their interpretations have proved to be so different and so little in agreement that they have been unable to reach the pastoral level. In like manner, a certain number of texts on this subject from the Fathers of the

pletely rejecting the interpretation proposed by Zoghby (p. 233). A polemic followed publication of this letter and A.-M. Dubarle attempted to put the matter in proper focus in *Rev. Sc. phil. et théol.* (July, 1966).

[3] This question had come under fire at the time of the Reformation. The Reformers—since they admitted only two sacraments: baptism and the Lord's supper—had in great part rejected the habitual conclusions of the Western theologians concerning marriage and, following Erasmus, interpreted Matthew 19, 9 in a sense favorable to remarriage in case of adultery. Among the best informed controversialists who have ably defended the classic Catholic thesis since the Reformation, we must mention Tournély, "An matrimonia solvantur per adulterium?" in his *Institutiones theologicae. Tract. de Matrim.* (Paris, 1757), pp. 533ff., which has provided the inspiration for the most recent theologians, generally speaking. We should note once for all at the beginning of this article the most recent as well as the most accessible work on the theology of marriage which might be consulted in order to complete what is said here: P. Adnès, *Le Mariage* (Coll. Le Mystère Chrétien. Théologie sacramentaire) (Tournai, 1963). Unfortunately, we were able to consult this work only when the present article had already been written, but we found therein confirmation, if not of our conclusions, at least of much of our information. On the other side, there is an excellent study of a modern Reformed theologian concerning this question: J. von Allmen, *Prophétisme sacramentel* (Neuchâtel, 1964), Ch. 6: "Le remariage des divorcés d'après le N.T.", pp. 183-211.

[4] Cf. J. Bonsirven, *Le Divorce dans le N.T.* (Tournai, 1948), and above all (one who cites the others) J. Dupont, *Mariage et Divorce dans l'Evangile* (Bruges, 1959), pp. 81ff. One of the conclusions which, since the publication of this work, has seemed to us among the most ingenious is that of A. Dubarle, "Mariage et divorce dans l'Evangile," in *L'Orient syrien* 9 (1964), p. 70; according to this opinion the *porneia* envisioned by the Gospel must be understood not as a passing act of adultery but as a perduring situation, "a grave and prolonged case of misconduct" which compromises conjugal life for good.

Church (both Greek and Latin) have been studied on numerous occasions.[5] Most of the time, the only conclusion reached has been that the doctrine of the absolute indissolubility of marriage has been affirmed by them with such vigor as to render even well-founded contrary interpretations of their thought of little value in the whole of their teaching.

On the other hand, a constant tradition of the Greek Church, based on a very ancient custom attested (without necessarily being defended) by several of the Fathers, has admitted tolerance in this matter. Divorce with remarriage is still granted in that Church for reason of infidelity, but the application of such tolerance to other cases is generally considered to be abusive. The Orthodox justify the intervention of the Church in this case by having recourse to what they call the *economy,* a principle whereby the Church supplies deficiencies in difficult cases by extension of the powers she received from Christ.[6]

For her part, although the Western Church has in practice also experienced much variation concerning this point during the Middle Ages,[7] she has increasingly refused—to the extent that she became conscious of her magisterium—to allow any condescension in favor of the injured partner, whether or not it be based on the Matthean text in question. The Catholic Church

[5] Cf. the most important of these texts cited by Adnès, *loc. cit.,* pp. 59-69. See also the comments on these texts of R. Souarn, "L'adultère d'après les Pères," in *Dict. Théol. cath.* 1, cols. 475ff., and H. Crouzel, "Separation ou remariage selon les anciens Pères," in *Gregorianum* 47 (1966), pp. 472-94.

[6] The two causes recognized by the Greeks as dissolving marriages were death and adultery (*thanatos kai moicheia*) (Asterius of Amasea, *Hom. 19: P.G.* 40, col. 228). Added to these, shortly afterward, was "civil death", that is, entrance into monastic life and disappearance with the presumption of death after the lapse of a considerable period of time. Concerning the *economy,* cf. the pertinent remarks of A. Scrima in Wenger, *loc. cit.,* pp. 215-7.

[7] Cf. Vacant, "Adultère dans l'Eglise latin," in *Dict. Théol. cath.* 1, cols. 497ff., and the lengthy footnote 4 on p. 58 of the article by C. Journet, "Le mariage indissoluble" (which reviews with moderation the classical position of the controversialists) in *Nova et Vetera* 41 (1966). Above all, great profit will result from a reading of the most remarkable study of all on the evolution of the doctrine of marriage in the West by G. Le Bras, *Dict. Théol. cath.* 9, cols. 2123-2317.

clearly declares, following the elaboration of her theologians and casuists (at least from the 12th century on), against ever permitting any "divorce" or "matrimonial rupture"; she admits only separation, considering herself as having no power to "loose" in so holy a matter. In difficult cases she concentrates on another point—the value of the consent and pact of the spouses. After investigation, she decides for or against the existence of the juridic bond and eventually declares for nullity of marriage.

I

STATEMENT OF THE PROBLEM ACCORDING TO A TEXT OF ORIGEN

On what authority, therefore, has the Greek Church[8]—whose tradition is generally of great value—relied to pronounce divorce and put into practice the interpretation of Matthew 19, 9? Here we find ourselves involved in a matter in which it is impossible to separate several complex and, at first glance, apparently unrelated questions. They constitute widely different perspectives between the Eastern and Western traditions. To lose sight of this fact is to expose ourselves to an irreducible viewpoint and a disastrous division. Here we find the theological character and theology of marriage, second marriages, separation from bed and board, continence and virginity, monogamy and ecclesiastical celibacy as points to be considered in a way of looking at things which cannot be juxtaposed from one tradition to another. We must take pains to situate them.

Origen's long commentary on a page of the Gospel (precisely Matthew 19, 3-12) will serve as our point of departure and summary, for all or nearly all the themes are treated therein as well as the teaching of St. Paul.[9] It is impossible to give the text in full, but we must cite a few parts that form the "woof" of our

[8] The non-Byzantine Eastern Churches have also legislated concerning divorce (cf. Dauviller and De Clercq, loc. cit.: Nestorian, p. 99; Coptic, p. 108; Armenian, p. 111; Ethiopian, p. 121).

[9] Origenes Mattheüserklärung, ed. Klostermann and Benz, (GCG 10, 2), I, 2 (Leipzig, 1937), pp. 318ff. The passage commented upon runs for 42 pages (24 columns in Migne, P.G., 13, cols. 1223ff.).

problem. We shall begin by quoting the Matthean text and several other very important Pauline texts, for this is indispensable.

Matthew 19, 3-12: And there came to him some Pharisees, testing him, and saying, "Is it lawful for a man to put away his wife for any cause?" But he answered and said to them, "Have you not read that the creator, from the beginning, made them male and female, and said, 'For this cause a man shall leave his father and mother, and cleave to his wife, and the two shall become one flesh?' Therefore now they are no longer two, but one flesh. What therefore God has joined together, let no man put asunder." They said to him, "Why then did Moses command to give a written notice of dismissal, and to put her away?" He said to them, "Because Moses, by reason of the hardness of your heart (*sklerokardia*), permitted you to put away your wives; but it was not so from the beginning. And I say to you that whoever puts away his wife, except for immorality (*porneia*), and marries another, commits adultery; and he who marries a woman who has been put away commits adultery." His disciples said to him, "If the case of a man with his wife is so, it is not expedient to marry." And he said, "Not all can accept this teaching, but those to whom it has been given. For there are eunuchs who were born so from their mother's womb; and there are eunuchs who have made themselves so for the sake of the kingdom of heaven. Let him accept it who can."

1 Corinthians 7, 1-2: It is good for man not to touch woman. Yet, for fear of fornication (*dia tas porneias*), let each man have his own wife, and let each woman have her own husband.

1 Corinthians 7, 5-9: Do not deprive each other, except perhaps by consent, for a time, that you may give yourselves to prayer; and return together again lest Satan tempt you because you lack self-control. But this I say by way of concession, not by way of commandment. For I would that you all were as I am myself; but each one has his own gift from God, one in this way, and another in that. But I say to the unmarried and to widows, it is good for them if they so remain, even as I. But if they do not have self-control, let them marry, for it is better to marry than to burn.

1 Corinthians 7, 38-40: Both he who gives his virgin in marriage does well, and he who does not give her does better. A woman is bound as long as her husband is alive, but if her husband dies, she is free. Let her marry whom she pleases, only let it be in the Lord. But she will be more blessed (*makariotera*), in my judgment, if she remains as she is. And I think that I also have the spirit of God.

1 Timothy 3, 1-2. 12: This saying is true: If anyone is eager for the office of bishop (*episkopēs*), he desires a good work. A bishop, then, must be blameless, married but once. . . . Deacons should be men who have been married but once.

Explaining Matthew 9, 2-12, after commenting at length on the two accounts in the text of Genesis concerning man and woman (1, 27 and 2, 23-24), Origen briefly sets forth the theology of marriage such as it is willed by Christ and with reference to Ephesians 5, 25 ("Husbands, love your wives, just as Christ also loved the Church"), to which he returns several times in his treatment. Then in his customary manner he widens the scope of his thought to include the whole of the scriptures and dwells on the infidelities of the synagogue who put to death the very one she awaited as her spouse after first spurning him.[10] In the Matthean clause—except for *porneia* (19, 9)—he sees a prophecy of the apostasy and rejection of Israel, and in the rest of the discourse of Christ the announcement of a regeneration and new nuptials. He goes on to remark that the "hardness of heart" (*sklerokardia*), cited by Jesus as the reason why Moses had tolerated divorce, has not failed to leave some trace, some "analogue" (*tis analogos*),[11] on the new economy. The spouse—

[10] *Origenes* . . . , *loc. cit.*, n. 16, pp. 321-4.
[11] *Ibid.*, n. 23, pp. 339ff.

as he has explained many times elsewhere[12]—although she is beautiful, has retained her baseness.

He notes that St. Paul permitted widows to remarry: "A woman is bound as long as her husband is alive, but if her husband dies, she is free. Let her marry whom she pleases, only let it be in the Lord." Origen comments that Paul says this because of the existence of a certain hardness of heart (*sklerokardia*) and a certain weakness for those who cannot respond to a superior gift and be "more blessed" (*makaroteros,* to use the apostle's term).[13] In effect, St. Paul counsels widows to remain in their state; but if they cannot contain themselves, let them marry: it is better to marry than to burn. Whereas for those who are to be accepted in the hierarchy, Paul requires— and Origen is pleased to mention—that they have only one wife.[14] *Sklerokardia* plays no part in their case.

Still following the apostle, Origen next speaks in the same regard to spouses who desire to abstain for a time in order the better to devote themselves to prayer. They can do so, but they should be careful not to frustrate themselves in a dangerous way. He adds that this is again written out of the reason of hardness of heart (*pros ten sklerokardian*), or again—as he explains elsewhere—out of condescension.[15] Furthermore, Paul himself comments on his opinion, saying, "I would that you all were as I am myself"—that is, free. But not everyone can accept this counsel.[16]

A bit later, Origen arrives at the question that will occupy us and that has already been the object of discussion many times.[17]

Moreover, it has happened that even some leaders of the Church—despite what we find written—have permitted a woman to marry even when "her husband is still living".

[12] For example, *Homélies sur le Cantique des Cantiques* I, 6 (Sources Chrét. 37) (Paris, 1954), pp. 71ff.

[13] *Origenes . . . , loc. cit.,* n. 18, p. 328.

[14] *Ibid.,* n. 22, p. 338.

[15] *Ibid.,* n. 23, pp. 339-40.

[16] *Ibid.,* n. 18, p. 328.

[17] *Ibid.,* n. 23, pp. 340-1.

They have done so in spite of the fact that it is written that "a woman is bound as long as her husband is alive" and "the woman who gives herself to another man while her husband is alive must be treated as an adulteress"; however, they have not done so without foundation (*ouk alogos*).[18] Indeed, it seems that [the leaders of the Church] tolerated this weakness (*sumperiphore*)[19] to avoid greater evils, despite what has been commanded from the beginning and written in the scriptures.

All the cases mentioned by Origen can be arranged according to various degrees:

1. At the top is the most perfect degree—to imitate Paul who, following Christ's indication, renounced the use of the flesh "for the kingdom of heaven" (Mt. 19, 12). There is no *sklerokardia* here. We know that Origen aspired to this perfection more than he should have, taking the Gospel phrase much too literally by a voluntary mutilation for which he later blamed himself.

2. Below this comes total monogamy, the same monogamy which—without being imposed on all—is required for members of the hierarchy and never admits of second marriages (no *sklerokardia*).

3. In third place is the case of spouses who, in the interests of an approved temporary continence, cannot (first appearance of *sklerokardia*) out of an excessive zeal expose their partner to danger.

4. In fourth place we must mention the case of widows who (second instance of *sklerokardia*) find themselves in second mar-

---

[18] An expression repeated by the Greeks at the Council of Florence and translated into Latin at that time by *non sine justis causis* (Hardouin, *Conciliorum Collectio* IX [Paris, 1714], pp. 431-2).

[19] We hesitate to translate with P. Crouzel (*loc. cit.*, p. 476), from whom we have otherwise drawn several fine translations, the word *sumperiphoram* as "liaison" in this case, although that would be more in harmony with the context and the word can have this meaning. Other places in Origen invite us rather to conserve for this term its usual meaning of *weakness* or *condescension*. We are indebted to our colleague D. M. Van Parys for this precision. It was also in this way that the old Latin translator of the 6th century had understood it (*P.G.* 13, cols. 1245-1246 at the bottom). The translation of Huet (*alieno arbitrio*) reproduced by Delarue (*ibid.*, col. 1246B) bypasses the difficulty and can lead to error.

riages which, it is important to note, do not have an incontestable sacramental quality in the Eastern tradition (even nowadays).[20]

5. Finally, there is the case which is acknowledged to exist (third *sklerokardia*) without being judged worthy of recommendation, yet all the more excusable although it is little in harmony with the scriptures: the case of the abandoned spouse toward whom the leaders of the Church show themselves somewhat tolerant. We should make mention of the curious fact that the text of Origen—although he is commenting on Matthew 19 —makes no allusion to the Matthean parenthetic clause (except for *porneia*), and nowhere gives this as the reason why remarriage has been permitted. No explanation is adduced.

Below this last degree we once again reach the level of the ancient Mosaic divorce, that is, divorce for whatever reason— the *sklerokardia* of Matthew 19, 9—which is no longer permitted since mankind has been raised up from its sin and Christ, restoring the pristine state, has become its bridegroom. Henceforth, his nuptials are the type and the model of all conjugal union as well as—in the same line although surpassing it— virginity consecrated by a more intimate union with him.

II

THE EASTERN TRADITION

If we refer to the Eastern Church tradition, we will see that this gradation is still present therein in almost the same proportions. True, we can perceive a modification in the fact that the superior degree of the priesthood—the episcopate—can no longer be conferred on a married man, and that the bishop must be a monk. But apart from this point, everything remains: transcendence of monachism over all other states; conjugal life permitted for members of the hierarchy with the exclusion of second marriages; transcendence of monogamy which, although by way of concession tolerates second marriages and only with severity

---

[20] This was equally contested by many Latin theologians in the Middle Ages. Cf. Le Bras, *loc. cit.*, cols. 2143ff.

third marriages, completely rejects fourth marriages; tolerance for abandoned spouses (although extended through abuse to other cases). The East has always rigorously maintained itself in the same line and has given it a robust quality against which all attempts at change have failed.[21]

The Western practice has evolved differently, although it partakes of very similar facts;[22] herein lies the difficulty of understanding it. Virginity has preserved its character of primacy, and all the clergy, including deacons—at least until Vatican Council II, which represents a very great change on this point—is vigorously obliged to celibacy.[23] All marriages after the first, although regulated by a reduced ritual and submitted to certain canonical reservations, have for a long time been allowed without restriction as to number,[24] and their sacramental character has not been contested. Finally, all divorce has been rejected, after a lengthy period of fluctuation in practice during which it never had the force of law, and only the separation of spouses is recognized as legitimate. As the laws concerning divorce have multiplied in civil legislation—that is, practically speaking, since the 19th century—the East has extended to numerous cases the ancient divorce which was recognized and limited by tradition, while the West for its part has progressively multiplied declarations of nullity.

We might well be surprised at not finding in Origen's scheme of things a place allotted to the Pauline privilege (when one of

[21] Recent tendencies on the part of the Orthodox, however, urge manifestation of more tolerance. At the inter-Orthodox Conference of Vatopedi in 1930, reforms had been envisaged concerning "second marriages of clerics, the marriage of bishops", etc. (*Irenikon*, 1931, p. 103.) Since then, these propositions have been taken up again many times, but not even the least decision has ever been made.

[22] Cf. the gradation given by Le Bras, notably with reference to St. Augustine, *loc. cit.*, col. 2126.

[23] The first Council of Orange (Can. 22) in 441 no longer admitted that deacons could be ordained if married. Cf. Hefelé-Leclercq, *Histoire des Conciles* II, p. 445.

[24] Their value was imposed in the profession of faith submitted to Michael Paleologus after the second Council of Lyons in 1274 (Denzinger, *Enchiridion*, ed. 1960, n. 465) and previously in 1245 (*ibid.*, n. 455) under Innocent IV to the Greeks of Cyprus.

the partners is not baptized), which a modern reader would probably seek to introduce as a supplementary *sklerokardia*. We shall see further on that Cajetan was troubled by this privilege. But for Origen, in this case, there is no true marriage "in the Lord".

The apostle is speaking of married people only insofar as both husband and wife are believers. He does not include among them all the others who form a disparate yoke. This is evident since he adds: "To the others, I say, not the Lord" (1 Cor. 7, 12). Are not these others married? He does not regard them as married, for in their case the wife is not joined to the husband by God. "For the others," he says, "it is not I who legislate but the Lord." [25]

This enables us to understand why in the Eastern tradition—of which Origen is the precursor—the union of man and woman has, since the time of Ignatius of Antioch,[26] been looked upon as effected by the Church which intervenes through her blessing, without reference to the contractual element. On the other hand, whenever this question has been discussed by the Doctors of Western theology, the simple contract between the spouses has been adjudged the instrument through which the sacramental grace has been conferred between Christians, and the contracting parties have been viewed as the ministers.

Thus the ever-increasing difference between the two conceptions is visible: the Eastern tradition tending to relate everything to the aspect of the mystery and the scriptures (while necessarily interpreting Matthew 19, 9 widely), and the West, on the contrary, fixing its attention on another aspect and ultimately

[25] Elsewhere in Origen's works we find allusions to the Pauline privilege, but in these places he also judges that if the spouses are not both believers there is no true marriage. Cf. H. Crouzel, *Virginité et mariage selon Origène* (Bruges, 1963), pp. 145-6.

[26] *Ad Polycarpum* V (Sources Chrét. 10) (Paris, 1945), p. 139. Cf. the testimonies in L. Goderfroid, "Le mariage au temps des Pères," in *Dict. Théol. cath.* 9, col. 2104. The marriage contract, the consent and its conditions, its value, etc., are all questions which remained outside the perspective of the Fathers. "They wished to consider marriage only in its natural dignity" (*ibid.*, col. 2114).

terminating in the consideration of the contractual element as
the basis on which grace has come to be conferred. If the Eastern
tradition (especially the Russian) has varied on this question
over the course of recent centuries, the reason has been due in
part to the influence of Latin theology, which on this point has
been abandoned nowadays by its theologians.[27]

Some have thought that the Greek Church had interpreted
Matthew 19, 9 in a wide sense in order to adapt herself to the
imperial laws that recognized divorce. "Never," it has been written, "did the Byzantine Church consider the Matthean text as
containing the exclusive reason for divorce; she saw therein the
application, under the aspect of an example, of the reasons
admitted by civil law. For it is through civil law that divorce
entered into the Byzantine Church. This is explained by the
dependence which the bishop of Constantinople—who owed the
independence of his See to the proximity of the *basileus*—mani-
fests toward the secular power." [28]

The Greek controversialist, Peter Arcudius (d. 1633), who
was little inclined to follow his ancestors and his predecessors in
theology, contested this explanation, citing precisely Origen's
reference to the excessively lenient prelates.[29] It was not at all a
question then "of the Byzantine Church", and besides, as we have
said, no allusion was made to the Matthean text by Origen to
justify these prelates. Therefore, we are in the presence of a
custom in vogue well before the Christian emperors in an age
when the Fathers were in no way obliged to submit to monarchs
for anything.[30]

Although transcendent monogamy can be considered as one
of the major innovations of the evangelical law, we must not be
too surprised by the fact that it encountered difficulty in being
really understood in its origins, or in being observed in all circles

[27] Cf. Jugie, *Dict. Théol. cath.*, *loc. cit.*, col. 2322 (corrected by P.
Trembelas, *Dogmatique de l'Eglise orthodoxe catholique* III (in Greek)
(Athens, 1961), p. 344 (French translation in course of publication).

[28] Dauviller and De Clercq, *loc. cit.*, p. 85.

[29] *De Concordia Ecclesiae occidentalis et orientalis* (Paris, 1626), 517D.

[30] On this subject, see the pertinent reflections of A. Scrima already referred to (*cf. supra*, n. 6).

—in the face of Jewish and pagan customs. The evangelical laws have wavered. In the Sermon on the Mount the aphorism concerning divorce and *porneia* is immediately followed by the prohibition against taking oaths: "But I say to you not to swear at all; neither by heaven . . . nor by the earth . . . nor by Jerusalem" (Mt. 5, 34). Indeed, taking an oath was often regarded as a sin in the ancient Church;[31] yet today it is no longer looked upon as such, since it is required in many circumstances by ecclesiastical laws. Doubtless, we cannot compare the two cases since the text of the Sermon on the Mount does not lack for differences—for example, it admits of no exception for swearing—but we can allow a certain period of time before this difference was uncovered.

Who could be surprised that Matthew's words "except for *porneia*" (5, 32 and 19, 9) would one day be used to justify not only separation but also remarriage when resignation to such *sklerokardia* was necessitated? The argument did have its force. There are other cases in the history of the Church wherein a text of scripture has been used to bolster an established tradition, even though no reference was made to the text in the beginning. In the present case, it was necessary that the sublime Pauline teaching on monogamy and its mystery, with reference to Christ and his Church, should have time to penetrate minds and hearts. It is by no means temerarious to believe that beginning at some epoch the Matthean clause (19, 9) was used to comply with the imperial laws concerning easy divorce, although we might lack proof of the moment of its insertion. However, we must recognize the fact that a more ancient tradition—perhaps close to the age of the apostolic Fathers—has prevailed in the East and has always been respected without receiving formal approbation: consent was given and then one day the tradition was validly supported by scripture. Such a manner of acting is difficult to stamp out since it is considered akin to a right.

We can see traces of this tradition in the testimonies of the

---

[31] Cf. the testimonies cited by Cornelius à Lapidé, "In Matth. 5, 32" in *Curs. Script. Sacr.* (Paris, 1868), Vol. 15, p. 169.

Fathers in conformity with Origen's assertion concerning the tolerance of certain prelates. Origen most probably represents the Palestinian tradition, possibly that of Egypt. About 150 years after Origen we find in Epiphanius of Salamis and Basil allusions to similar traditions which probably refer to Cyprus and Cappadocia.

1. In an oft-quoted passage Epiphanius makes only a veiled reference to the Matthean text (we might say he goes beyond it):

He who has only one wife will be advantageously praised and honored among members of the Church; but not he who has not been able to be content with one who has died, or whom—although a separation has taken place for reason of fornication or adultery or some other cause—the divine Word (*o theos logos*) does not accuse and does not exclude from the Church or from life but tolerates because of his weakness. The reason is not so that he might have two wives at the same time, the first being still alive, but so that, separated from her, he might be licitly united to another if the case should present itself; for the holy Word and the holy Church have pity on him, especially if such a man is otherwise devout and living in accord with God's law.[32]

Although this text might be pleasing to some, it is highly disturbing. On the one hand, Epiphanius speaks of other causes besides adultery. We are here in all likelihood in the presence of cases established by civil legislation. The Roman laws expurgated by Christianity admitted as cause for divorce only the crimes of poisoning, homicide (or infanticide on the part of the woman), and violation of graves (or procuring). Previous to this Christian expurgation of the laws, Origen had already mentioned two of the same causes as graver than adultery,[33] but he considered them as nothing more than reasons for separation, and he did not speak of remarriage as Epiphanius does.

On the other hand, Epiphanius appeals to the "divine Word" in a sense that goes beyond that of Matthew 19, 9, since other

---

[32] *Adv. Haer.* 59, 4, Edit. of Holl, II (GCS, 25), pp. 368-9.
[33] *Origenes . . . , loc. cit.*, p. 342.

causes are listed whereas the Gospel text envisions only one. It has been suggested that this is a reference to the mercy of which St. Paul gives proof in several places (notably those cited above by Origen apropos of *sklerokardia*).[34] In any case, the custom envisaged by Epiphanius, which is not formally opposed by him, is here the object of clear testimony.

2. Basing himself on another custom rooted in civil law, which obliged the husband to put away his adulterous wife— although the man who sinned with an unmarried woman would not incur this penalty (inequality of man and woman)—Basil of Caesarea explains his point of view concerning the woman living with the betrayed husband who is thus reduced to being separated from his wife. "As far as the woman is concerned," he says, "who is living with a husband who has been abandoned, I do not know if one can (*ouk oida ei dunatai*) call her an adulteress, for it is the one who has repudiated her husband who will be accused as such." [35]

Canonical penalties existed for adulteresses.[36] Basil questions their validity in such a case. He does not justify the case, but his text is another witness for the tolerance of an accepted usage. Moreover, a few lines later he states: "As for the one who has been abandoned, he is excusable, and the woman who lives with a man in such a situation is not condemned."

Other texts could also be adduced in favor of the Greek tradition. Many of them—as also those of Latin writers—have often been interpreted by controversialists as justifying merely separation from bed and board. We have retained only those texts that can clearly imply remarriage.

[34] Crouzel, *loc. cit.*, p. 486.
[35] *Letter 188*, Ed. Courtonne (Coll. Budé) (Paris, 1961), p. 128. Concerning the opinions of St. Basil, we possess an excellent article of F. Cayré, "Le Divorce au IVe siècle," in *Echos d'Orient* 23 (1920), pp. 303ff. We could cite many texts here, but we have given only the most characteristic one (Can. 9 of the first canonical letter).
[36] And even for second marriages. Cf. B. Kotting, "Zu den Strafen und Bussen für die Wiederverheiratung in den fruhen Kirche," in *Oriens Christianus* 48 (1964), pp. 143-9.

III

THE WESTERN TRADITION

Lists of witnesses have also been drawn up from Latin patristics. We can list them only in summary. The first one we shall cite—because it recalls the position of St. Basil which we have just treated—is a passage of St. Augustine in his *De fide et operibus* (written in 413), which undoubtedly represented a tradition prevalent in Africa, although this is not explicitly stated. Moreover, Augustine is an acknowledged defender of the indissolubility of marriage.

> The man who puts away his wife taken in adultery [the text is concerned with accession to baptism] and marries another should not, it seems, be equated with those who put away their wives and remarry outside the case of adultery. In the divine scriptures (*sententiis*), it is not at all clear (*obscurum est*) whether the person who is permitted without any doubt to put away his adulterous wife is himself to be considered an adulterer if he marries another, and in my opinion he commits a pardonable error (*venialiter*).[37]

However, the text that deserves to be cited first in the Latin tradition is a passage of Ambrosiaster, a work that is generally believed to have been written at Rome in the second half of the 4th century. The relevant sentence (*Comm. in 1 Cor. 7, 10*) is, as we have seen in Basil, based on the legal inferiority of women and the inequality of the spouses, still deeply rooted in the customs of the period.

> It is not permissible for a wife to leave her husband because of fornication or apostasy . . . for the inferior cannot at all use the same law as the superior. . . . But it is permissible for a husband to take another wife when he has put away his sinful wife, because the man is not bound by the law in the same manner as the woman. For the husband is head of the woman.[38]

[37] C.XIX, n. 35: *P.L.* 40, col. 221.
[38] *P.L.* 17, col. 218. This text of Ambrosiaster, summarized by Gratian

This passage of Ambrosiaster refers, through the preceding line, to the Matthean clause where Christ is alluding to the man who wishes to put away his wife (reply to the question of the Pharisees).

These two texts of Augustine and Ambrosiaster by themselves show that *in Africa and Rome—no more than in the East—no legislation had been passed in the 4th century in favor of a rigid interpretation of Matthew 19, 9. Why these two traditions later underwent such wide differences remains to be explained.*

The first indication of a strict legislation expressed in writing is found in Spain at the Council of Elvira in 306. Its canons carry penalties against women who marry another after leaving their husband because of adultery on his part.[39] We should note, however, that it is still a question solely of the woman. Shortly afterward, in 314, the Council of Arles substantially repeats the interdiction; however, when applied to the man, it is no more than a counsel;[40] this shows that the tolerance still existed.

On the other hand, the African Councils of the 5th century, in any case from 416 on,[41] condemn all remarriage while the partner is alive, and we find the same prescriptions in one of the acts of Innocent I in 417.[42] True, it is not a case of formal adultery, but the basis is there for a disciplinary rule which will gradually no longer admit of exception. While the Byzantine East will hardly see any more regional councils, since everything is placed in the hands of the emperor, the West will find occasion for a multiplicity of local legislation over several centuries, which will eventually snowball into canonical collections. Thus, laws will progressively be established in the Gallic and the other

---

(d. 1179) (C.17.C.XXXII,9,7: ed. Friedberg, I, col. 1144), is rejected by him as an apocryphal text of Ambrose, and is inserted in a series of chapters which take violent issue with every lenient interpretation of Matthew 19, 9. Its influence on subsequent canonists has been considerable, as we shall see further on.

[39] Can. 9: Denzinger, 52a.
[40] Can. 10, I: Hefelé-Leclercq, *op. cit.*, I, p. 287.
[41] Council of Milevis, Can. 10: Mansi, *Concilia* IV, p. 331.
[42] *Ibid.*, III, p. 1049.

northern regions, although many cases will be found still stamped with the ancient gropings.

All this has been established a great many times by the authors,[43] who have gone to much trouble to reduce almost to nothing the argument favorable to remarriage in case of adultery —referring either to the insertion of the Merovingian laws or their routine sequels in the law of the Church, or to other justifications. However, they have not succeeded in explaining all of them.[44]

Although we see the legislation become established along strict lines at the Councils of Nantes in 658,[45] Hereford in 673,[46] and Friuli in Aquilea in 791,[47] the Penitential of Theodore of Canterbury (d. 690) allows remarriage to the husband whose wife has misbehaved—clearly stipulating that this holds good "only if she was the first wife"—while the reverse (remarriage for the injured wife) is not tolerated. Theodore was Greek and he referred to the text of Basil which we cited above. On the other hand, the Councils of Verberie in 756[48] and Compiègne in 757[49] allow remarriage in case of incestuous adultery on the part of the guilty

[43] Cf. Vacant, op. cit., p. 488 and passim, and Adnès, loc. cit.

[44] The most certain judges in this matter—as often in others of the same kind—are the editors of the ancient texts. The erudite Jacques Petit (17th century), the editor of several canonical editions, cites, after the Council of Arles (cf. supra, footnote 40), the text of a Roman Penitentiary favorable to the remarriage of an injured partner (P.L. 99, col. 1057); he notes that according to the bishops of this period the matter was thus not considered absolutely prohibited. Cf. the lengthy annotations of Petit on this question (ibid., cols. 1150ff.). The same observation is made by Bignon (1613), editor of the formularies of Marculf (P.L., 87, col. 746), declaring that remarriage had been at times tolerated even then, despite the laws of the Church. The same is true of Fr. Petau, S.J. (d. 1652), editor of St. Epiphanius, who recognized the faculty of the separated partner to remarry for a legitimate reason (P.G. 41, col. 1023); the same holds for Fr. Sirmond, S.J. (1651), editor of St. Avitus, the bishop of Vienne in Gaul (d. 520), who recognized the same right in case of fornication (P.L. 59, col. 267).

[45] Hefelé-Leclercq, op. cit., II, p. 298.

[46] Ibid., III, p. 920.

[47] Ibid., III, p. 1094.

[48] C. 18, ibid., p. 920.

[49] C. 11, ibid., p. 942 and passim.

husband. As for the Capitularies of Charlemagne, they adhere to the strict formula.[50]

A little later, the Councils of Germany, particularly the one at Tribur (in the region of Mainz) in 895, have a detailed legislation that shows both the primitive state of morals and the efforts of the Church to provide some remedy for it.[51] Moreover, still other councils and canonical texts testify that the preservation of conjugal life was at that time the great concern of the Church. But a century later, the preoccupation must have changed because the Gregorian reform concentrated all its attention, in matters of matrimonial law, on ecclesiastical celibacy.[52]

This was also the age of great canonical collections which had a decisive influence on the interpretation of laws and whose importance we will establish. We refer notably to those that concern our subject: the collections of Réginon of Prumm (about 906), Bishop Burchard of Worms (about 1023) and, above all, Gratian who about the year 1150 composed his *Concordantia discordantium Canonum* which was to enjoy the highest authority over the course of the following centuries. Gratian showed himself to be the declared adversary of all lenient interpretation of possible remarriage after adultery.[53] But the sometimes altered previous collections—notably that of Burchard, which served as a norm until the 15th century in certain Germanic lands—reproduced without comment the texts in the other sense, such as those of the Councils of Verberie and Compiègne, which seem to have been used for a long time afterward as references.[54]

Beginning with the 13th century, Latin theology rallied around Gratian's opinion in an almost general manner, and his interpretations thus attained the force of law. These were to be set in opposition to the usages of the Greeks, with whom scarcely any relations were maintained, in the manner of truth to error. Further, in the question of divorce, theologians began to assert

[50] C. 43: *P.L.* 97, col. 166.
[51] Hefelé-Leclercq, IV, pp. 697ff.
[52] Le Bras, *op. cit.*, cols. 2133-2134.
[53] C. 16-18, C.XXXII Q7. Ed. Friedberg, I, cols. 1144-1145.
[54] *P.L.* 140, cols. 819-821.

that in accord with an ancient formula, when one of two scripture texts was more clear (in this case, the text of St. Paul) and the other less clear (the Matthean clause), the less clear passage must be explained by the more clear one and the question was not to remain open.

Nevertheless, *in the official documents of the Roman Church of that period which concern the Greeks, no mention is made of divorce.* It is not mentioned in the letter of Innocent IV for the Greeks of Cyprus which nonetheless recommended many Latin usages,[55] or in the profession of faith imposed after the Council of Lyons of 1274 on Emperor Michael Paleologus; the profession is content to state in a general manner that it is not permissible for husbands to have several wives at the same time or for wives to have several husbands.[56] At the Council of Florence, when the question was proposed at the very last moment by Pope Eugene IV after the decree of unification had been signed, the Greeks answered that if they sometimes allowed divorce, this was not without reason (*ouk alogos*)[57]—we recognize Origen's formula herein—and the matter was not pushed any further.

IV

THE COUNCIL OF TRENT AND THE SUCCEEDING PERIOD

The Council of Trent inherited the task of establishing the Catholic teaching on marriage in a definite manner. But we know that Canon 7 of Session XXIV, which prohibited divorce

[55] Denzinger, nn. 449ff. Modern canonists cite one text much less than the old canonists—the famous reply of Pope Alexander III to an *Episcopum Vicentinum* (1170) according to which it is clear that a bishop, after pronouncing the divorce before the ecclesiastical assembly, had also in the 12th century allowed remarriage to a person whose husband had been outside the country for more than ten years and even after being warned had not returned. Interrogated about this, the pope was content to legitimize the children without expressing himself further (*Decretales of Gregory IX,* L. IV, vol. 17, c. 8. Ed. Friedberg, II, col. 712).

[56] Denzinger, n. 465.

[57] Cf. *supra,* footnote 16. Hardouin gives the complete text of the answer.

"for any reason", thus summing up the general opinion of theologians since the 13th century, was submitted to a revision precisely because of the custom of the Greeks.[58] The matter has been recalled several times in the last few years.[59] The Venetian ambassadors to Trent rejected the excessively absolute formulation of the teaching on divorce because they claimed it would be very difficult to apply in the isles of their most serene republic, in which dwelt many Greeks who followed their ancient customs, at least insofar as divorce was concerned.[60] After various revisions the *canon was consequently modified, but just enough not to affect the Greek usage.*[61] *Thus respect was shown to an immemorial custom,* without in any way further incriminating the ancient Fathers who had refrained from condemning it in an absolute manner.

The post-Tridentine theologians have sought—in opposition to the Protestants—to draw from the context a formal dogmatic declaration. However, one of the greatest teachers, Cardinal Cajetan who knew of the controversy of the Reform but who died before the Council (1534), had put forth an opinion with his usual freedom of judgment. This opinion never failed to impress later generations and also recalled in a certain sense the position of Basil as well as that of Augustine in the face of the difficulty of interpreting Matthew 19, 9. It compares the Matthean clause (19, 9) with the Pauline privilege which grants dissolution of the bond between non-baptized persons when one of them enters the Church (1 Cor. 7, 12ff.). Cajetan's manner of understanding St. Paul is certainly much different from Origen's, for whom, as we have said, the apostle spoke in his own personal name. Here is his argument:

[58] Denzinger, n. 977.

[59] Cf. especially J. Dupont, *op. cit.,* pp. 115ff.; R. Laurentin, *Bilan du Concile, IVe session* (Paris, 1966), pp. 87ff.

[60] Ehses, editor of Volume IX of the *Conciliorum Tridentinum* of Goerresgesellschaft, reproaches Massarelli, secretary of the Council, for having deliberately omitted (*consulto, ut reor*) from his valuable *Diarium* several points, which it would have been useful to retain, concerning the proposition of the Venetians (p. 686, n. 3).

[61] Cf. Denzinger, n. 977, footnote 1, which on the other side cites Pius XI, *Casti connubii,* confirming the opinions of modern theologians.

I am not only astonished (*miror*) but stupefied (*stupeo*) at the fact that although Christ very clearly excepted the cause of fornication, the torrent of the Doctors does not admit this freedom on the part of the husband [to take another wife]. Paul, on the other hand, by a word that is less clear, admits that the nuptial bond can be broken by a cause other than the one cited by Christ as the sole exception. Since I believe that an ancient usage of the Church has authorized this sense of the text in question (*communem firmatum*) and that this text is susceptible of such a sense, we must maintain that in the Gospel the Lord did not give the law of freedom to the two spouses but to the husband, as the text clearly states. Paul, on the contrary, has promulgated a law of freedom for both partners by an authority which is certainly divine. And I say this in answer to the question posed by the opposition of the teaching of Paul and that of Christ. Christ indeed excepts only the case of fornication; Paul teaches something else, indicating that fornication is not the only cause.[62]

True, the opinion of Cajetan—whose reputation has always been highly respected in Latin theology, especially among Thomists—has been judged a bit bold; besides, the woman was in his day still treated as inferior; hence it has been generally surrounded by prudential circumlocutions—*pace tanto viro*—in order not to be accepted. All the same, it merited citing.

However, after the Council of Trent, when parts of the Eastern Churches that had broken away from their groups of origin joined the See of Rome, efforts were made to have them renounce their custom on this point.[63] Prior to this, the Decree *Ad Armenios* at the end of the Council of Florence[64] expressly mentioned the prohibition of remarriage on the part of the injured partner, and this Decree was also imposed on the united Syrian Jacobites.[65] Yet, each time that it was necessary to evalu-

---

[62] *Epist. Pauli et aliorum Apostolorum* (Paris, 1542), pp. 123-4.

[63] This took place progressively in several places. The Wallachians and Ruthenians of Transylvania retained their custom of remarriage in case of adultery up to the 19th century (Vacant, *loc. cit.*, p. 505).

[64] Denzinger, n. 702.

[65] *Ibid.*, n. 714.

ate the ancient tradition in all its force, the custom was respected, at least up to a point, as we have seen at the Council of Florence and even at Trent.

Indeed, there is little chance that it can ever be otherwise. The hesitations that we have seen in Origen (*ouk alogos*), St. Basil ("I do not know if one can"), St. Augustine (*obscurum est; venialiter*), and Cajetan (*miror et stupeo*) could always be repeated and extenuate the absolute demands of those who would condemn the Eastern tradition, even if it remains disputable. The two traditions have evolved within frameworks that are too different to be capable of juxtaposition.[66] An effort must be made to understand each and to refrain from imposing the viewpoint of one on the theological and canonical development of the other.

Everyone is agreed in condemning divorce as an evil in itself and in regarding as an act of great virtue on the part of the separated partner the fact of sacrificing himself or waiting for the return of the other despite any consequences—whether fortunate or unfortunate—that can be foreseen. But the "hardness of heart" (*sklerokardia*) does exist and will continue to exist for all time.

In the past, the reflection made by an Edinburgh journal in 1830, on the occasion of a letter of Pius VIII, has been cited; the letter dealt with the indissolubility of marriage, and the journal, after an elogium of the Catholic teaching, added:

> In our country, when a husband no longer desires his wife or a wife her husband, they simply have themselves taken in flagrant adultery in order to withdraw from the conjugal yoke and form a liaison more to their liking. It can be just

[66] Father Yves Congar has recalled (*Inform. Cathol. Intern.*, October 15, 1965, p. 30) how one of his Anglican friends, Canon Douglas, who was one of the best authorities on the Eastern Churches, had one day said to him "that it was this in his opinion [*divorce and remarriage*] which represented the greatest difficulty forming the obstacle to a union". Our colleague D. C. Lialine (d. 1958), who had lived in Russia a long time and knew the Orthodox very well, often repeated the same thing to us. This holds good only in the hypothesis of a refusal "to understand the other"; such an understanding can become possible today. But where will we find a legislator astute enough to refrain from new abuses?

and reasonable to free the injured partner from a pact that has been violated and dishonored by the other contracting partner, but it is absurd, and more than absurd, to make a crime the means of attaining freedom.[67]

V

CONCLUSION

We believe that it is this danger which has caused and continues to cause Catholic theologians to hesitate to reopen the parentheses of the Matthean clause that have been so tightly closed for so long and to show themselves favorable to a modification of the law along the Greek lines. The Greeks on their side have multiplied the case of divorce with remarriage by applying the law far beyond the Matthean exception. We shall not go into these cases here,[68] all the more so since we on our part have an equivalent today, a phenomenon of which we have no right to be proud: the increasing number of requests for annulment to the Roman Rota; this fact has disturbed Pope Paul VI, who recently voiced his sorrow in a speech to the workers of the Tribunal of the Rota on January 25, 1966.[69]

On his side, the Greek Orthodox Metropolitan of the two Americas issued a statement last June revealing the same disquietude in his Church: "The bonds of marriage," he declared, "must be reinforced." Then, recalling that in the past Orthodox ecclesiastical tribunals often granted religious divorces to couples that had obtained civil decrees, he acknowledged that this manner

---

[67] Cited in Perrone, *De Matrimonio*, n. 133 (ed. Migne: *Theol. Curs. Compl.* 25, pp. 278-80. It concerned the encyclical *Traditi humilitati* at the beginning of the pontificate of Pius VII; cf. *Bullarii romani continuatio* (Prati, 1856), Vol. IX, p. 26.

[68] Cf. Dauviller and De Clercq, *op. cit.*, pp. 84ff.; C. Vogel, "La legislation actuelle sur les fiançailles, le mariage et le divorce dans le royaume de Grèce," in *Istina* (1961-1962), pp. 174ff. See also A. Wenger, *op. cit.*, pp. 243ff.

[69] The February 20, 1966 issue of *Doc. cath.*, p. 307, which "subtitles" the paragraph in question: "A cry of alarm over the multiplication of reasons for nullity of marriages."

of acting is not healthy for society, and furthermore that it represented an obstacle to conversations with Rome concerning unity. "That is why," he concluded, "from now on divorce will be granted by an ecclesiastical tribunal only for very specific reasons which a special commission is presently determining. This represents on our part an important ecumenical effort." [70]

These words of Metropolitan Jakovos offer encouragement. An effort must be made on the part of all Christians to purify themselves, each in his own tradition, but we should do it together. In this matter as in many others, nothing will be done as long as Christians do not think in terms of "East and West" instead of thinking of one against the other. We must not forget that in the matter that concerns us the left hand must—by reason of *sklerokardia*—from time to time not know what the right hand is doing.

The real remedy—but is it applicable to anyone else except the elite?[71]—is the reevaluation of the sublime Pauline and patristic theology of marriage, as has been successfully attempted by certain groups for several years. We have been surprised to discover the great dogmatic riches contained in the ancient marriage rituals among Eastern Churches (Coptic, Byzantine, Ar-

[70] According to the July 15, 1966 issue of *Inform. cath. intern.*, p. 17, the Orthodox author who has recently contributed the most toward raising the ideal of Christian marriage is Professor P. Evdokimov in *Le Sacrement de l'Amour* (Paris, 1962).

[71] We might note here under the category of general information that the famous American ethnologist, Margaret Mead, who was at the Church and Society Conference of the World Council of Churches at Geneva in July, 1966, put forth a solution in an interview (cf. *Reforme*, August 6, 1966, p. 11) which she believed might be approved by the Protestant Churches; it specified a period of life in common that could be easily canceled by the spouses, enabling them to determine whether they are capable or not of always living together and rearing children. The religious marriage effected at the end of this probationary period would be quasi-irrevocable. We could also refer to the conclusions of the study of J. J. von Allmen cited at the beginning of this article. We must recognize that many young people marry nowadays with very little awareness of the profound realities of the natural and supernatural psychology of married life, although the role of the Christian laity is to cause to shine forth in "the modern world" the noble ideal of monogamy instituted by Christ.

menian, Syrian, Maronite and Chaldaic).[72] No doubt, when these rituals were composed, a corresponding catechesis provided a lengthy preparation for the future spouses, for it is compressed in the details of several ceremonies.

A very great faith is necessary—at every level—for us to live our Christianity in an ardent manner. The tendency to fall is such a part of our nature that if this faith is not sustained by a vibrant sacramental life, association and constant application of the love of Christ through observance of his Word—and on the part of spouses by a continuous vigilance to maintain fidelity at its highest plateau, no matter what happens—the precautions taken by the laws are futile.

[72] Cf. A. Raes, *Le mariage dans les Eglises d'Orient* (Chevetogne, 1959).

John M. Oesterreicher/*Newark, N.J.*

Yes, No, and Nevertheless

Catholic and Protestant Comments on the Conciliar Statement concerning the Jews

In the introduction to his most recent book, *The Church and the Jewish People,* Cardinal Bea writes: "The *Declaration on the Relationship of the Church to Non-Christian Religions* . . . has been widely acclaimed as a milestone in the history of the relations between the Church and the Jewish people." [1] But now and then, the "Jewish Statement",[2] particularly in its final version, encountered vehement, even scathing criticism. In the following pages, I shall make it my task to gather significant opinions by Catholics and Protestants and examine their value. Limitations of space, however, permit only selections from the abundant material.

I

CATHOLIC COMMENTS

The prevailing response of Catholic authors is positive. As he reflected on the significance of October 15, 1965—the day the Council fathers settled the arguments for and against the Declara-

[1] A. Bea, *The Church and the Jewish People* (New York, 1966), p. 7.
[2] "The Section of the *Declaration on the Relationship of the Church to Non-Christian Religions* That Deals with the Jews" would be the correct term, but it is unwieldy. Hence, I shall refer throughout this paper to the "Jewish Statement" or simply to the "Statement" or the "Declaration".

tion by their definite vote in its favor—Abbé Laurentin, one of the most judicious reporters on the Council, reminded readers of *Le Figaro* of his observation the year before that this text—compact, clear and truly speaking to the men of our times—might well be one of the most beautiful achievements of Vatican Council II. He assured his readers that he stood by this remark, despite the changes made in the final version.

These were his words: "The text is still beautiful. It resembles one of those women who continues to be admired though her beauty has begun to fade, those who knew her before whispering, 'If only you knew *how* beautiful she was!' That open smile with which the Church had, at a moment of exceptional grace, looked upon the people from which she sprang, has now been replaced by a somewhat forced attitude. Some feel keenly the stiffness [of the final version]." [3] Yet, one should not be too astonished at the changed tone, Laurentin went on; the Statement was, after all, a first attempt. Moreover, the separation of the Church from her Jewish roots was a rift that went back to the days of her youth—the protoschism. Once one has been made aware of it, he finds this initial wound, which has never healed, in every century in ever new and unexpected forms. We must now take upon ourselves the pain first suffered by St. Paul: so deep was his anguish that he wished "to be an outcast for the sake of [his] brethren" (Rom. 9, 3). [4]

Manfred Plate, editor of *Der Christliche Sonntag,* understands the Council as a self-examination of the Church. In his book, *The Council as a World Event,* he regards the section on the Jews as the core of the entire Declaration. Christianity has gifts in common with the Jews in which the other religions do not share, namely "the revelations, promises and mysteries of the Old Covenant". [5] It is therefore incomprehensible, Plate concludes, that for centuries Christians inflicted so much suffering, so many wrongs, upon the Jews. Here, nothing must be glossed

[3] *Le Figaro,* October 16-17, 1965.
[4] *Ibid.*
[5] M. Plate, *Weltereignis Konzil: Darstellung-Sinn-Ergebnis* (Freiburg im Breisgau, 1966), p. 293.

over. The "Jewish Statement" demands that Christian-Jewish relations be radically changed. Never again must it happen that Christians persecute Jews. The Statement is for Plate "a very concrete mandate for the reform of preaching, catechetical work and piety. Every motive that could, in some manner or other, beget Jew-hatred must be totally extirpated".[6]

The renewal must not stop there, however, Plate continues; it must include the presentation of all saving events, of God's dealings with Israel and mankind. Whoever takes the Declaration seriously will no longer belabor the imperfection of the Old Testament as was done so often in the past. Nor will he look on it as antiquated, as finished and useless. Hence, the post-conciliar period must develop "a positive theology of the Old Testament",[7] one that underlines its intrinsic value.

The conclusion of Plate's essay strikes the right note so clearly, it seems to me, that I should like to quote it in full: "Finally, the conciliar Declaration has forever ended that sad period of Church history that knew crusades and religious wars. How much harm these wars have wrought upon religion! And in the name of God! With the words of the Gospel on the lips! Now the Council proclaims: 'The Church reproves as foreign to the mind of Christ any discrimination against men or harassment of them because of their race, color, condition of life or religion.' Only now, after a development of two thousand years, has Christianity at long last entered into a state of maturity. It has done so in unmistakable words, though it continues to bear the burden of a history—of popes and of laymen—who for centuries dimmed the purity and integrity of Christ's message. A mighty work of reform by Vatican Council II!" [8]

To make the present survey representative, at least to some extent, several American comments need to be recorded as well. Even more than the Europeans, commentators in the United States are preoccupied with the changes that appear in the final

[6] *Ibid.*
[7] *Ibid.*, p. 294.
[8] *Ibid.*

version of the "Jewish Statement". *America,* for instance, one of the leading Catholic weeklies in the country (edited by the Jesuit Fathers of North America), took a stand on these modifications in two successive editorials.[9] The author of the first found the reasons given for the omission of the phrase "guilty of deicide" unconvincing and the deletion of "condemns" disappointing, while other modifications of the Statement seemed to him a matter for discussion. Seen as a whole, however, he maintains that it is still "a good text"; indeed, it is "an excellent statement". The writer of the second editorial repeats the previously voiced scruples but stresses the fact that the Declaration—"one of the greatest and most promising accomplishments of Vatican Council II"—affirms the common spiritual patrimony of Christians and Jews, and also that here the Church solemnly decrees "that no basis exists in the religion of Christ for 'hatred, persecutions and displays of anti-Semitism' ".

Before the fourth session of the Council, the editors of *America* published a lead editorial in which they gave what appears to be their enduring point of view: "In the long run, the conciliar Decree will be judged not according to its success in meeting the varied and even contradictory demands of non-Catholics, but according to whether it gives expression to the awakening Christian conscience in these days of rejuvenation. . . . The Council's concern with the Jewish question, as Msgr. John M. Oesterreicher expressed it recently, is itself 'one of the fruits of the Pentecostal spirit astir in the Church: it is part of its movement toward renewal'. This new spirit moving through the Church is the best hope for an historic turning point. To quote Msgr. Oesterreicher once more, the Council's actions can 'put an end to the grave abuses of the past, when the cross, that majestic pillar of love, became a whipping post for Jews'." [10]

Another weekly, *Commonweal,* edited by laymen, took a similar position: "The final statement on the Jews was neither the best nor the worst of the various drafts to come before the Vatican Council. Nevertheless, it is clear and emphatic, and

[9] *America* (Oct. 16, 1965), p. 430; (Oct. 30, 1965), pp. 490f.
[10] *America* (July 3, 1965), p. 6.

should be of immeasurable help in tearing the roots of anti-Semitism out of Christian tradition." With these words the editorial comment, written shortly after the Council accepted the Declaration, begins. It continues: "Objections to the final statement, in the last analysis, are objections to the parliamentarianism out of which it came. A statement could have been imposed from above, as has happened in many a Council. In this one, the statements reflected consensus, and consensus always implies that the final product falls short of what the most enlightened of the drafters regard as ideal." Though the editors were "utterly depressed" by the tediousness of conciliar procedure and the resulting delay of decisions, as well as by the general weariness that it produced, their spokesman could thus conclude: "It is not accurate to say that the statement has been 'emasculated'. The statement is a fine one." [11]

In the same issue of *Commonweal*, there appeared one of the regular reports on the Council by Fr. Gregory Baum, one of the consultors of the Secretariat for Promoting Christian Unity, who played an important role in the realization of the Statement on the Jews. He rated the final version even more positively, if possible, than the editors: "If the present text had not been preceded by a previous one, it would have been judged as a great act of friendship. . . . In a few years the unpleasant modifications will be forgotten. The lasting result will be the education to respect and friendship with Jews which the Catholic Church gives her members through the present Declaration. The quasi-theological arguments used by anti-Semites have been once and for all refuted. The dogmatic foundation has been laid for spiritual brotherhood between Christians and Jews." [12]

II

PROTESTANT COMMENTS

Opinion of the Protestant world about the Declaration varies so much that it is not easy to draw a faithful portrait. One of

[11] *Commonweal* (Oct. 29, 1965), p. 112.
[12] *Ibid.*, p. 120.

the most refreshing voices is that of Pastor G. Richard-Molard, one of the official observers for the French Reformed Church. His commentary on the Council [13] stands out for its unspoiled vision as a view unshackled by the stereotyped reactions of many other critics.

It is not hard to imagine the history of a Declaration that for four years led a "nightly existence" and met with bitter opposition, Molard holds. While other conciliar texts were opposed by only one group of adversaries, the Statement on the Jews had the honor of facing a fourfold resistance. First and foremost were the conservatives who were against every schema that demanded even the slightest revision of past ideas or attitudes or, as in this instance, a break with a disastrous interpretation of scripture that had become routine. A second group, whose resistance, however, was political rather than doctrinal, consisted of the bishops from Arab countries. A much nobler opposition came from a third group: those who doubted that it was good theology to view the existence of the present-day people of Israel as a mystery engaging the Church. Inversely, one must not forget the small minority that insisted on giving the text a deeper theological structure.

It was only after having steered past a thousand reefs that the Statement became reality, Molard remarks. There were diplomatic pressures on the Vatican; there were anonymous inflammatory pamphlets that with deadly hatred called Cardinal Bea a "dirty Jew" and accused Pope John of letting himself be tricked by the "international organization of Jewish Freemasonry"; finally, there were the maneuvers within the Council that forced Cardinal Bea to make concessions. But these were not the only opposing forces. Orthodox Jewry rejected the Declaration from the very first as an intolerable paternalistic interference by the guilty Church in the life and freedom of Israel, the only People of God. Members of the extreme Right in all Western countries fought the document because hatred of the Jew is an important

[13] G. Richard-Molard, *Oui et Non—Un pasteur au concile* (Paris, 1966).

article of their "creed". Despite its essentially positive attitude
toward the Statement on the Jews, the Protestant world regretted
that, in the Declaration as a whole, the Jews appear on the same
plane as the other non-Christian religions. A greater drag than
all these oppositions was the mentality of the Christian people
whose soul is imbued with a latent anti-Semitism.

Even though this list calls for a few minor rectifications, I
shall desist from correcting it so as not to divert attention from
the following observation by Molard: "One could almost say
that the whole world was arrayed against it. This is, after all,
fully in accord with a millennia-old tradition of the 'elder people
of election', whose wayfarer-existence makes it a sign of contradiction to all the nations. . . ." [14] Molard thus sees in the resistance to the Declaration a protest against the existence of the
Jewish people, an existence that defies the laws of nature and
recalls that the Gospel, too, is, if not "against nature", at least
"against the tide". Before affecting Christian-Jewish relations,
the Statement ought, therefore, to serve as a reminder to Christians that "in this world they must be signs of contradiction,
strange beings whose hope obliges them to march counter to the
current of a world that runs without ceasing, subject to a fatality
it is powerless to contest". [15]

Whoever wishes to know what makes the Declaration so remarkable must read it, Molard writes. It is a document to which
one may say all possible "no's"—provided he reads it outside its
historical context. In that case, one will fail to notice what a
conversion it represents, even in comparison with the most recent
past. [16] Whoever reads it as he ought—that is, as the result of
pitiless strife and as the new beginning of a spectacular change
of the Church's attitude toward Israel—can only pronounce an
unqualified "yes".

Molard goes on to say that though "the text does not spell out
the Church's repentance for the crimes committed by her faithful
toward the Jews, it is nevertheless clear that this gripping and

[14] *Ibid.*, p. 90.
[15] *Ibid.*
[16] *Ibid.*

historically significant fact underlies all that the Declaration states".[17] "The Declaration will be good for nothing if it does not penetrate the mentality [of all Christians]. It will have been in vain if the Church now becomes satisfied with herself, though she should be ashamed to have taken so long to understand the Gospel [regarding the Jews and the place granted them in God's saving scheme]. The Church will not be able to prevent pogroms unless she concerns herself methodically with individual Christians." If the Statement is understood well, it cannot help but make individual Christians humble, indeed, servants of humility before Israel, the first People of God.[18]

A remarkable instance of consent is the public statement of the former Secretary General of the World Council of Churches, Dr. W. A. Visser 't Hooft. In mid-October (prior to the final vote on the Statement), he called it "a clear expression of the biblical truth which has been obscured in all Churches, namely, that it is through the Jewish people that the divine revelation has first come to men, and that the deep bond which thus exists between Jews and Christians must not only be a memory but a present reality. Anti-Semitism is, therefore, a denial of the Christian faith itself". The rejection of anti-Semitism by the General Assembly of the World Council of Churches in New Delhi in 1961, together with the Statement of Vatican Council II, seemed to him indubitable evidence that all the Churches now wish to reshape their attitude toward the Jewish people, and that they have thus begun to make amends for the many errors of the past.[19]

In the American biweekly *Christianity and Crisis*, George A. Lindbeck, the well-known Lutheran theologian who attended the first sessions of the Council as the official observer for the Lutheran World Federation, wrote: "The section on the Jews, contrary to what some commentators have suggested, does not arrogantly presume to 'absolve' but simply—though not as force-

[17] *Ibid.*, p. 92.
[18] *Ibid.*, p. 94.
[19] *The New York Herald Tribune* (Oct. 15, 1965).

fully as one could wish—warns against anti-Semitism." [20] Since this mistaken evaluation appeared under the heading "A Definitive Look at Vatican II", the author of these pages thought it his duty to correct Dr. Lindbeck's opinion. In a letter to the editor, he explained that the Statement was much more than a warning, forceful or not, against anti-Semitism. What the Council had done was to restate the Pauline vision of the mystery of Israel.

This assertion was followed by a "factual report", giving four perspectives: (1) The Church is dependent on the Israel of old. (2) God's love for Israel endures; neither his gracious gifts nor his calling is withdrawn. (3) The people he adopted as a son (Exod. 4, 22; Jer. 31, 20; Hos. 11, 1), to whom belong the covenants, the promises and the patriarchs, and of whom is the Christ, according to the flesh, is not rejected. (4) Christians and Jews have a common patrimony.

These viewpoints were authenticated by the corresponding passages of the Statement and by references to the epistle to the Romans. This seemed sober enough. But Dr. Lindbeck considered the answer "unbalanced" and "unqualifiedly enthusiastic". He wondered whether one's enthusiasm could be so unrestrained since the Statement had its obvious defects. First, the Statement "contains no words of penitence for Christian sins against the Jews"; secondly, "the restatement of the Pauline vision . . . loses much of its effect because Judaism is treated as just one of the non-Christian religions", a treatment "St. Paul would have found ludicrous, perhaps even blasphemous".[21]

Regarding the first objection: There are words and there are deeds of penitence. Though the word "atonement" is indeed missing from the text of the Declaration, the Declaration itself is, and must be seen as, an act of reparation. The Council could not make a global confession of guilt without running a serious risk. Its confession might have been mistaken for an acknowl-

[20] "A Definitive Look at Vatican II," in *Christianity and Crisis* 26 (Jan. 10, 1966).

[21] "Correspondence," in *Christianity and Crisis* 26 (June 13, 1966), p. 134.

edgment of certain theories on the origin of anti-Semitism, theories that simplify the complex reality of history. A differentiating statement on so delicate a matter, however, might have occasioned other misunderstandings, even unfriendly interpretations, such as those brought about by the distinctions that were incorporated in the final version.

The Council could hardly have ejected, through the front door, the devil of collective guilt of Jews and, through a side entrance, admitted the Beelzebub of the collective guilt of Christians. To be sure, as member of a family, community, state, or religious body, a man bears a certain responsibility for the acts of other members and of the group as a moral entity. What rabbinic tradition tells of the people of Israel we must state with regard to every community: its members are sureties, each for the other. But to bear co-responsibility is not the same as to bear guilt. Every man can, indeed ought to, beg God's forgiveness for the misdeeds of his fellows; he can, and ought to, help carry the burden of a sinning neighbor or sinning neighbors, but he cannot be contrite for their sins. Contrition is an eminently personal act. It would be unsound, indeed a gross misunderstanding, to confuse the mystery of human solidarity with that of guilt.

As for Dr. Lindbeck's second objection: Anyone who gives the entire Declaration but a cursory reading will get the impression that here a section is devoted to Judaism in very much the same way as other sections are to other religions, that here Israel is robbed of her particular character, her election. Yet, whoever reads the total document with care will soon discard this first impression as rash, as false. A comparison of only the preamble to the total Declaration with the paragraph introducing the section on the Jews shows plainly that no attempt was made to blur the essential differences between them. The preamble points to the modern milieu: Technological achievements and political reorderings have stripped the earth of its great distances, thereby transforming it into a settlement of neighbors. This proximity of alien cultures and their religions obliges Christians more than ever ultimately to open themselves to all that is true and good in them—that is, to God's activity everywhere. The preliminary remarks to the special chapter on the Jews, however, proceed not from a contemporary situation but from the fact that in probing the mystery of the Church, her mode of existence and her mission, the Council was necessarily made aware of the bond that unites the Church for all times with Abraham's stock. While the sections on the various religions of mankind praise the omnipresence of grace, seeing it at work all over the globe, the part devoted to the Jews celebrates the covenant fidelity of Israel's God.

That is all very well, some will counter, but the present frame was chosen not because of any sublime theological view, but rather in order to divest certain Arab charges of the least justification. This is true, but it is not the whole truth. The comprehensive frame owes its existence no less to the apprehensions of many Asian and African bishops that their non-Christian compatriots would feel aggrieved if the Council, brushing other religions aside, made Judaism the only theme of its Declaration. Is this not definite evidence, some will still ask, that the Council succumbed to the modern tendency to level all things, or that it was guided by mere expediency? Not at all; rather, it is proof that the Council was inspired by pastoral solicitude.

Be that as it may, it is dangerous to draw far-reaching conclusions from the circumstances that accompany the birth of a phenomenon. At no time does its genesis fully explain its meaning. In the present structure of the Declaration, the section on the Jews is an axis around which the other sections are grouped or, better still, the stem of a tree around which the other statements grew like branches. That the Jewish Statement, to change the image once again, could act as a crystallizing agent proves once more the divinely given function of Israel to serve and to prepare the world's salvation: "All the families of the earth shall bless themselves by you" (Gen. 12, 3), the Lord said to Abraham. The prophets in turn hailed Sion as the spiritual center not only of Israel, but of the nations, too, as the place from which the *Torah,* the manifestation of God's will, went forth, and to which, in the future, the nations will make their pilgrimage (Mic. 4, 1-2; cf. Is. 60). Through the vast structure of the total Declaration, this pilgrimage is somehow anticipated, just as God's salvific will for all is proclaimed anew. Vatican Council II has been called the end of the Counter-Reformation; our document spells rather the end of the Reformation. The question that moves us today is no longer: "How do I get a gracious God?" but rather: "How does God effect the salvation of every creature?" Jesus is not only the redeemer of those who accept him by faith; his redemptive work is so abundant as to make him the bearer of salvation even to those ready for his touch though they do not know him.

While I warmly approve of the all-embracing character of the Declaration, I do not mind saying that sincere men may well differ on it. No difference of opinion is possible, however, on the criticism made, among others, by the present Secretary General of the World Council of Churches, Dr. Eugene Carlson Blake, at a time when he was still the Stated Clerk of the United Presbyterian Church in the U.S.A. In a lecture before an American Jewish congregation, Dr. Blake declared: "The most disturbing thing to me about the whole discussion [at Vatican Council II] has been the assumption so widely held by Christians that it was in the power of the Church—any Church—to absolve the Jews from this ancient charge of guilt [for Christ's death on the cross]. Certainly, all Christians, if they thought about the whole matter, would agree that God alone is the judge of men, and that any usurpation of this prerogative of judgment is as great a sin as any it would presume to absolve." [22]

In this speech, the reference to the Council remained a bit veiled. Yet, an editorial in *The Christian Century*, an American weekly that calls itself ecumenical, was as plain as one could wish it to be: "If Jews, as some of the Catholic bishops hold, are guilty of deicide, then no council of bishops and no pope can absolve them. If Jews, as most of the Catholic bishops believe,

[22] *The New York Times* (Nov. 15, 1965); cf. "The Jewish Declaration," *Commonweal* (Dec. 7, 1965), p. 331.

are *not* guilty of deicide, are not to be held collectively responsible, in the 20th century, for the death of Jesus in the 1st century, then to speak of absolving them of a crime of which they are not guilty is to exhibit not merely faulty diction but also a brutally unjust spirit. . . . What monstrous arrogance is this which assumes that Christians have the right and the power to forgive or not forgive Jews for a crime of which they are not guilty! . . . This talk about absolving the Jews is worse than nonsense; it is a crime against the Jews, a sin against God." [23]

Was there ever a greater waste of passionate words over nothing? There is not even a hint of absolving the Jews in the "Jewish Statement". The expression, no doubt, originated among harassed editors who, because of the limitations of space or because of theological ignorance, invented eye-catching headlines such as: "Council Absolves Jews." One is thus compelled to assume that the author of the editorial had not properly read the Declaration and that he based his condemnation, not to say slander, of the Council on newspaper headlines which no experienced reader takes seriously. There is bitter irony in this: a man who castigates the Christians of the past because they treated the Jews recklessly is himself thoughtless enough to speak—without reason—of "the height of Christian insolence".

It is incomprehensible that anyone should so misconstrue the work of the Council. No great theological formation is necessary to discern the tremendous difference between an alleged act of forgiveness, by which the Council tried to clear the Jews, and the service it actually rendered—its earnest endeavor to eliminate forever from the Christian consciousness any "anti-Jewish" interpretation of scripture. It is no less comprehensible how the above misconstruction found one adherent after another. One of the several imitators is Rabbi Maurice Eisendrath who, in a programmatic address to a convention of the Union of American Hebrew Congregations, urged the participants to repeat, "in dignity and candor", the verdict of *The Christian Century*.[24] True dignity and

[23] "Christian Insolence Reaches New Heights," in *Christian Century* 82 (Sept. 29, 1965), p. 1181.
[24] "The State of Our Union," Message of the President (The Union of American Hebrew Congregations) (New York, 1965), p. 21.

real candor would demand that these critics—who by now must have realized how unfounded their accusation was—revoke their charge. As far as I can see, this has not yet been done.

My anxiety for historical accuracy and my respect for Dr. Blake's courage move me to record a quite different utterance made in the same speech mentioned above. In contrast to those who see none but the sins of Christians, he found it in himself to make this frank observation: "Both Christians and Jews have used their faith in God as an excuse for religious prejudice and persecution. While it is true that in quantity the persecution of Jews by Christians is overwhelming, it needs to be remembered that in quality this persecution is not different from that visited upon the first Christians by Jewish religious leaders." [25]

I wish Dr. A. Roy Eckardt, professor of religion at Lehigh University and editor of the *Journal of Bible and Religion,* undoubtedly the most caustic of all Protestant critics of the "Jewish Statement", had shown himself as intrepid as Dr. Blake. But in a two-part article, "End to the Christian-Jewish Dialogue", which appeared in *The Christian Century* in the spring of 1966, he calls the struggle for the Statement "the recent tragedy at Rome". The final (in his opinion, "watered-down") version is the "triumph of minority dictation". The majority succumbed to this dictation because it suffered "a failure of nerve". "How did it happen," Dr. Eckardt asks, "that despite their protracted and courageous fight for an unequivocal declaration in the spirit of Pope John, the bishops and experts of the Secretariat for Promoting Christian Unity, custodians of the schema, had to yield to top-level pressure and resign themselves to the wording of the final draft?" Simply, he answers, because "the anti-Semitic virus is a chronically nagging presence in the Christian corpus".

In Dr. Eckardt's vocabulary, the "anti-Semitic virus" is the view that "the Jews" said "no" to messianic salvation, that they "rejected" Jesus as their messiah. Everyone who denies them the praise they deserve for their "objective [sic] obedience to the Word of God in an unredeemed world" proves himself, accord-

[25] *The New York Times* (Nov. 15, 1965).

ing to Dr. Eckardt, an anti-Semite. Thus, he is emboldened to assert that the New Testament "contains the beginnings of anti-Semitic hostility". He then goes on: "As long as the Church continues to stand up to 'read the Word of God', she has to accept the consequences. She must find that certain 'lessons' in and of themselves sustain and propagate a derogatory image of 'the Jews'." [26]

As a typical example Dr. Eckardt cites 1 Thess. 2, 14-16, a passage that incidentally is not one of the pericopes of the Roman liturgy and could therefore not have incited the faithful to hatred of the Jews. Admittedly, the apostle's language here is cutting. His heart aches because the young community of Thessalonica is in pain. The Thessalonians endure the same torments from their countrymen that the Jewish Christians of Judaea had to bear from theirs. Paul does not call the persecutors of Judaea by their proper names. He does not single out King Herod and the priestly clan in Jerusalem as the originators of the persecution (cf. Acts 8, 1ff.; 12, 1ff.)—something we modern men would have liked to see. He simply says "the Jews" and adds, in deep anger, "who killed the Lord Jesus and the prophets and drove us out". They displease God and are hostile to all men, he exclaims, for they try to keep the apostles from preaching the Good News to the Gentiles. Thus they make full the measure of their sins and call down upon themselves God's wrath. When he wrote to the Thessalonians, Paul did not measure his words with a precision instrument, nor did he do so when he professed to the Romans his passionate love for Israel, when he offered himself to God as a victim for the sake of his brethren (cf. Rom. 9, 1ff.). A noted exegete has rightly called the impetuosity with which the apostle repudiates his kinsmen in this passage the reverse of the burning desire with which he embraces them in the epistle to the Romans.[27]

The reproaches the apostle here heaps against the Jews are not an essential part of the epistle; they are parenthetical—clear

[26] *The Christian Century* 83 (March 23, 1966), p. 362.
[27] B. Rigaux, *Les Epitres aux Thessaloniciens* (Paris, 1956), p. 445.

proof that they sprang from a sudden upsurge of emotion, from a heart that smarted with grief over the continuing hindrance of his apostolic activity. Such explanations, however, will not impress Dr. Eckardt who refuses to look at the realities of history. The responsibility for the early conflict between the infant Church and the Judaism of those days rests for him with the Christians, and the Christians only. Thus, he speaks of the "immorality of so many of the recorded sentiments of New Testament writers" which the majority of Christians today will not admit. And so he carries on: "Because we [Christians] are unprepared spiritually to live with the elements of anti-Semitism in our own scriptures, we have to try to tell ourselves that they are somehow not there. The result is moral illusion, moral entrapment. Anti-Semitism remains the bloody brother of anti-Judaism."

Dr. Eckardt neither inquires into the causes of those New Testament texts that show opposition to the Synagogue nor does he seek ways that will prevent their being made to serve hostility against Jews. Again, he does not "let on" that nowhere does the New Testament bear more distinctively Jewish features than in those passages that launch into "anti-Jewish polemic". I am putting this phrase between quotation marks because I consider it, despite the frequency with which it has been used for a century or so, a poor choice. The struggle was, after all, one among Jews and, for that matter, not the only one of its kind.

Why, for instance, does Dr. Eckardt fail to compare the language of the New Testament with that of the desert scrolls? The men of the Qumran Brotherhood called their Jewish adversaries who did not embrace their interpretation and observance of the *Torah* "sons of darkness" (1 QS I, 10), "liemongers", "prophets of deceit" (1 QH II, 31, IV, 9f.), "dissemblers", "prophets of falsehood" (1 QH III, 28; IV, 13), etc. In contrast to the New Testament, the monks of Qumran pledged themselves without mercy "to hate all the sons of darkness, each according to the measure of his guilt, which God will in the end avenge" (1 QS I, 10), to bear unremitting, nay, eternal hatred toward the men of perdition and to have no traffic with them (1 QS IX, 22). Further, why is there not the slightest suggestion in Dr. Eckardt's article that it was no less a lover of his people than Moses who in the Old Testament called Israel "rebellious, defiant toward the Lord" (Deut. 9, 7), indeed, that it is God himself who complains "how stiffnecked this people is" (Exod. 32, 9). Why does he keep from his readers the fact that in the whole New Testament there is no reproof that equals Isaiah's denunciation of Israel's unbelief (Is. 1, 22ff.)? The passionate language that marks the conflict between the early Church and the Synagogue is thus nothing less than a prophetic legacy.

Quite probably, it has never dawned on Dr. Eckardt that such "reserve" falsifies the facts and retards the deepening of Christian-Jewish co-existence. It robs biblical Israel, moreover, of one of her glories. In her ranks there were always men of conscience, men of God who dared to confront the mighty ones and their flatterers. Any appeal—overt or concealed—which seeks to eliminate all laments, rebukes and calls for repentance—in short, the prophetic tradition—from the New Testament is a disservice to Christians as well as to Jews. Only the Christian who sees his own face, whenever he looks at those whom Christ and the apostles censured and summoned to an inner conversion, will meet his Jewish brother with that humility which is indispensable to the renewal of Christian-Jewish relations.

I have treated Dr. Eckardt's negative stance so extensively because it is typical of a small minority which believes it can win the goodwill of Jews through "self-abandonment". In a sort of masochistic determination this minority thinks that spiritual suicide of Christians is the only genuine answer to, and the only genuine act of reparation for, all the sufferings inflicted upon Jews, particularly those of Auschwitz. Neither a morbidly excessive self-accusation nor a denial of "the Christian 'claim' to be the true religion" (in Dr. Eckardt's eyes "claim" is an un-Christian word) will have a wholesome effect on Christian-Jewish relations; both attitudes are themselves in need of a physician.

They are a menace because they may prevent Christians from *engagement* in the work of true reparation, a work so urgently needed.

Dr. Eckardt's voice is not the voice of the evangelical world. For example, near the end of his by no means uncritical review of the "Jewish Statement", the German Evangelical-Lutheran pastor J.-Ch. Hampe writes: "On the day of the decisive vote, Cardinal Bea reminded us of the parable of the mustard seed— an instance, by the way, of the absorption of Jewish wisdom into Christ's proclamation of the Gospel. Cardinal Bea thought of the 'passion' of this small conciliar text whose fate, thoughts and words betrayed a phenomenal growth. But one could apply the parable to the future of the Declaration, too; it has entered the world modestly, but it will teach an increase of faith and may yet become the biggest tree in the garden, among whose branches the birds roost. . . . In the end—so the Christian as well as the Jew knows—things will be as in the song of King David: 'Weeping may lodge with us in the evening, but in the morning there is singing and joy' (Ps. 29 [30], 6)." [28]

III

Two Advancing Contributions

It is not enough to refute Dr. Eckardt's nihilistic criticism of the Jewish Statement with rational arguments—in other words, to set opinion against opinion. On his obituary notice of the Christian-Jewish dialogue ought to follow, I think, tokens of new life, signs of a new vision of the roles assigned to the Church and to Judaism. Thus, I would like to conclude my survey with thoughts from the essays of two Catholic authors who advance and make fruitful the pronouncements of the Declaration.

In a special issue of *Esprit,* Joseph Hoffmann professes that for him as a Catholic the Statement is part "of that movement which humbly places the Church under the authority of God's

[28] "Ergänzungsheft zu Eckert-Ehrlich," in *Antisemitismus—Schuld der Christen?* (Essen, 1966), p. 34.

Word so that she may in all things that make up her most intimate and essential life find herself again".[29] For the first time in history, we stand today before a positive view of Judaism by the Church.[30] In the course of her self-reflection, of her becoming alive to her nature as the People of God, she could not help but encounter the mystery of Israel and rediscover it at the very center of her recollection.[31] One can say, Hoffmann repeats, that in some way "the Church has found again the fullness of her memory".[32]

Hoffmann believes that the Statement will undoubtedly be helpful to an authentic conversation between Christians and Jews. What this conversation will be like, however, and where it will lead us no one can predict today.[33] Its starting point is undoubtedly our common patrimony. There will be no confrontation of truths, no facing each other by the partners of the dialogue, but rather a common look at the common inheritance which Hoffmann sees, above all, as the undivided cleaving to the living God who reveals himself to us. The dialogue will thus be—nay, must be—a witness before the world. This does not mean a common front of the "spiritual forces" against materialism but, much more radically, a common testimony to the insufficiency of the world and the absoluteness of God. Here, Hoffmann maintains, "the Church and the Jewish people have one mission".[34]

Another essay on the Statement that points toward the future is by Dr. Kurt Schubert, professor of Jewish Studies at the University of Vienna. He stresses that the Statement on the Jews does not mean a reduction of the Christian message; far from being shortened, the message is deepened.[35] By its very introduction, Schubert states, the Statement on the Jews holds an exceptional

---

[29] "Vatican II et les Juifs," in *Esprit* 34 (June, 1966), p. 1156.
[30] *Ibid.*, p. 1168.
[31] *Ibid.*, p. 1169.
[32] *Ibid.*, p. 1170.
[33] *Ibid.*, p. 1166.
[34] *Ibid.*, p. 1170.
[35] K. Schubert, "Die Erklärung des 2. Vatikanischen Konzils über der Juden," in *Bibel und Liturgie* 1 (1966), p. 16.

position: the crucial point here is the mystery of the Church, the bond that ties the people of the new covenant to Abraham's stock.[36] Hence, Schubert feels justified in saying: "The Jewish religion is therefore not a non-Christian religion like any other; rather, it is founded upon the same covenant and the same promises we ourselves are. In a certain sense, Judaism is more than a non-Christian religion, for there exists not only an *ecumene* of the confessors of Christ but also one of the confessors of the covenant. Judaism is thus an essential element of the ecumenical conversation among separated Christians . . . for the affirmation of Abraham's call and Israel's election [as expressed in the conciliar Statement] . . . is the foundation on which the Christian faith rests" [37]—and with it, the ecumenical dialogue.

Schubert recalls that the Statement stresses emphatically Israel's enduring acceptance by God. Despite Jerusalem's short-sightedness that prevented her from recognizing God's presence in Jesus, Israel continues to be God's beloved. This statement broaches, according to Schubert, "a theological topic that is of decisive significance for the Christian-Jewish dialogue, as well as for the inner-Christian reflection on Israel: the question of whether the covenant [with Israel] was abrogated or not".[38] In order to clarify the problem, Schubert points first to the unparalleled challenge the person of Jesus was to his contemporaries. In him there came forward one who had power over sickness and death; but rather than abolish sickness and death themselves, he only cured and revived individuals. In him there appeared one who preached the nearness of God's reign, without, however, bringing about the great eschatological change Judaism awaited. Though for the faithful the time of God's reign has indeed dawned, its final realization is long in coming.[39]

Schubert asks: "What light do these thoughts throw on the problem of the revoked or unrevoked covenant of God with

[36] *Ibid.*, pp. 19f.
[37] *Ibid.*, p. 20.
[38] *Ibid.*
[39] *Ibid.*, p. 21.

Israel?" [40] In answer to his own question, he states: "We [Christians] must, first of all, profess that we, too, still await the parousia of Christ, in the fullest sense of the word. The petition of the Lord's prayer, 'Thy kingdom come', has lost nothing of its immediacy or topicality. As long as sin, death and sickness are not universally overcome, the promises that envision a state in which they are conquered still stand. In this sense Israel's waiting is legitimate; in this sense we may speak of a Jewish-Christian *ecumene* of those who have hope. In this sense—and only in this sense—can we properly speak of an unrevoked covenant." [41]

For Schubert, such an understanding of the reality of Israel's covenant and the importance of eschatological hope means also an enriched grasp of what it means to be a Christian. Jews and Christians, both professing the living and holy God, though separated in their beliefs, ought to realize their oneness in the hope for the "time of refreshment", "of universal restoration" (Acts 3, 19f.). Aware or not, they are part of the *ecumene* of hopers. This depth perception makes us realize the salvatory place (*den heils-geschichtlichen Platz*) the Jewish people holds in the "interim", the time between the first and the second coming of Jesus. Thus Schubert has shown to theology a new point of departure, a new course, and held out to the conversation between Christians and Jews the prospect of great promise and fruitfulness.

[40] *Ibid.*
[41] *Ibid.*

PART III
DO-C DOCUMENTATION
CONCILIUM

Office of the Executive Secretary
Nijmegen, Netherlands

Andrew Greeley / *Chicago, Illinois*

Some Results of Catholic Education in the United States

While Vatican Council II had encouraging words to say about worldwide Catholic education, it must be confessed that the document was none too specific about either the problems of Catholic education or the expectations that can be legitimately felt for the results of formal education. Unfortunately, at the present time research in the area of Catholic education is hardly beyond the embryonic stage. There is simply no way of knowing whether observations that can be validly made about Catholic education in one part of the world would continue to be valid if applied to Catholic schools in other parts of the world. The need for cross-cultural and worldwide research on the subject of Catholic education is obvious, and it is to be hoped that with the passage of time such cross-cultural research will become possible and, indeed, mandatory.

Until very recently little in the way of concrete social research had been done about the world's largest Catholic school system —that of the United States of America. However, in recent months two reports have been issued from extensive research projects, both of which were financed by the non-Catholic Carnegie Foundation. One project was carried on at the University of Notre Dame under the general direction of Dr. George N. Schuster, the assistant to the president of that university. The other project was under the direction of the present author and

163

his colleague, Dr. Peter H. Rossi, at the National Opinion Research Center (NORC), University of Chicago. Two projects can only be considered a beginning of serious Catholic educational research in the United States, but they do represent a comprehensive beginning and enable us to make some fairly safe generalizations about the impact of Catholic education in this country.

The Catholic school system in the United States is so large that even most American Catholics have a hard time comprehending its size. Almost seven million young Americans are in Catholic schools, and one out of every six Americans of school age is attending a Catholic school. The Catholic school system of the archdiocese of Chicago is the fourth largest in the country, and the combined systems of the archdiocese of New York and the diocese of Brooklyn would constitute the fifth largest system. (The three largest are in the public schools in New York City, Los Angeles and Chicago.) In addition to the thousands of primary schools and secondary schools, American Catholicism also maintains over 300 accredited colleges and universities and a vast number of scholasticates and seminaries. For example, within the territorial confines of the archdiocese of the Chicago Standard Metropolitan Statistical Area (the diocese of Chicago and Joliet), there are more than thirty institutions which purport in some fashion or another to offer higher education.

American Catholic education, therefore, is a vast, amorphous, very loosely organized collection of systems which educates more than two-fifths of the Catholic children in the country (and one-sixth of all the children). It has been constructed almost entirely out of the donations of the Catholic faithful, with only small amounts of government money being used for such purposes as dormitory construction at the colleges and universities. Given the fact that until very recently the Catholic population was made up for the most part of poor immigrants and their working-class children, some of the efforts of Catholic education must be rated almost incredible. It still remains to be asked, however, how this system came to be and what the impact has been on the lives of American Catholics.

While the history of American Catholic education has yet to be written, there is every reason to think that our Catholic schools had their remote origins in the "hedge schools" of 18th-century Ireland. In Ireland of the penal times the government-controlled schools were viewed both by the British and by the Irish as means of winning away Irish children from the absurd superstitions of the Roman Church. Even though it would appear that Irish faith and Irish nationalism frustrated these purposes, it was not nearly so clear to the Irish of the penal days that their children would be able to resist what they (the Irish) thought were the insidious attacks on any Catholic doctrine. Therefore, informal Catholic schools were organized by the laity and the clergy to provide some kind of education in Catholic religion, in addition to or as a substitute for what was taking place in the school system. On occasion, at least, some of these schools were conducted outdoors near the hedges which line the Irish country roads, whence came the historic name of "hedge schools".

When the Irish came to the United States, they began with a serious suspicion of the common school, both because of their experiences in Ireland and because of what they took to be the rather obvious Protestant tone to education in the common schools. When attempts to work out some kind of compromise with the common or later the public schools failed (whereas in Canada the attempts were successful), the Irish turned to establishing their own separate Catholic school system. The basic argument was similar to that used in Ireland. In the absence of Catholic schools the faith of the immigrant children would be in serious jeopardy in an unfriendly proselytizing Protestant-controlled public school.

The idea of a separate Catholic school system was reinforced in later years when other immigrant groups came to view the separate school system as a way not only of preserving faith but preserving at least some semblance of old country culture in the

New World. Thus, the German and Polish groups, particularly in the Middle West, were strongly in favor of a parochial school system and bitterly resented the attempts of Archbishop John Ireland of St. Paul to work out some sort of accommodation between the Catholic and the public school systems. Even though Ireland's efforts received a *tolerari potest* from Rome, the opposition of anti-Catholic elements in the population doomed the experiment to failure.

Non-Catholic Americans ultimately determined that religious education could be carried on outside of the formal school system, but Catholics, since they inherited the idea of separate schools from their European backgrounds, chose rather to unite religious training with the other elements in formal education. Even though it may no longer be necessary to maintain a separate school system in order to protect the faith of the children of the immigrants (if, indeed, it ever was necessary), American Catholicism is strongly committed to its school system, and despite criticism that we will mention later in this article, there is no evidence of substantial retreat from the principle of separate Catholic education.

Before we discuss the question of the impact of Catholic education, we should first say a word about who attends the Catholic schools. Many Americans had felt that since Catholic education was primarily a result of the immigrant experience in this country, with the waning of the immigrant experience Catholic education would decline as a formal system. Thus, it would have been predicted that the well-to-do and better educated Catholics would be less likely to send their children to Catholic schools than poorer and less educated Catholics. However, the two research projects under discussion discovered exactly the opposite. There is a direct relationship between social class and attendance at Catholic schools. Thus, the more education a parent has and the higher his income, the more likely he is to send his children to a parochial school. Furthermore, since American Catholicism is essentially a big-city religion, the churches in the large metropolitan regions are more likely to have the resources necessary for Catholic education. Hence, big-city Catholics are more likely to attend Catholic schools. Finally, the Irish, in great part the founders of American Catholic education, are more likely than any other group to be involved in Catholic schools. Thus, half of the graduates of Catholic colleges alive in the country today are of Irish ancestry and 40 percent of those who graduated from Catholic colleges last year are Irish, even though the Irish only constitute one-fifth of the Catholic population in the country.

It is a commonplace in the American Church that the majority of the Catholic children are not in Catholic schools, but this assertion should be qualified by two comments. First of all, only about 65 percent of American Catholics desire any sort of formal religious training for their children. Secondly, perhaps 15 percent more of the American Catholic population would send their children to Catholic schools if they were not in regions of the country where there are not enough Catholics to support such a school system. Thus, it would be a mistake to assume that Catholic schools are turning away many applicants or that there exists any alternative which will reach the one-third of Catholic children whose parents do not seem to be inclined to provide any formal religious education for them. It is, therefore, more of a missionary than an educational problem that is under discussion when it is observed that more than half of the Catholic children in the country are not in parochial schools.

Do Catholic schools have an influence on the religious behavior of adult Catholics? As Table 1 shows, they do indeed have an influence—and a statistically significant influence—on church attendance, reception of the sacraments, religious knowledge and ethical and doctrinal attitudes. Whether the percentage differences in the table are impressive or not depends upon one's point of view. In most social research the differences of the magnitude presented in Table 1 would be considered important. Researchers who are somewhat skeptical about the power of formal education to notably change behavior patterns which children have learned from their home and family (and most of those

TABLE 1

RELIGIOUS BEHAVIOR AND PERCENT ATTENDING EACH SCHOOL

Religious Behavior	School Attendance			Gamma Associa- tion
	All Catholic	Some Catholic	No Catholic	
High on sacramental index[c]	37	24[a]	14[b]	.26
High on accepting Church as teacher[d] .	46	35[a]	31[a]	.15
High in doctrinal orthodoxy[e]	33	24[a]	17[b]	.19
High in ethical orthodoxy[f]	35	28	23[a]	.12
High on religious knowledge index[g] . .	26	22[a]	13[b]	.30
N	345	699	796	

[a] Significantly different from "All Catholic".
[b] Significantly different from "All Catholic" and "Some Catholic".
[c] Mass every week; communion several times a month.
[d] Accepting Church's teaching authority in four or more areas.
[e] Four or more orthodox responses.
[f] Eight or more orthodox answers.
[g] Three or more correct answers.

researchers have this skepticism) would view the percentage differences in Table 1 as being, all things considered, rather impressive. On the other hand, those critics, as well as supporters of Catholic education, who have until now expected that Catholic schools could be required to turn out large numbers of "fully developed" Christians, would consider that the data presented in Table 1 indicate some kind of major failure of Catholic education. One is free, of course, to choose whichever position one wants to take on the matter, but it should be noted that, at least from the point of view of social research, the expectations that formal education will notably change the values and behavior patterns of young people must be considered rather naive.

Thus, the present writer and his colleagues concluded that while nothing in the data presented in the table, as well as the vast amounts of other data reported in our work, would force us to conclude that Catholic schools had indeed been essential for the survival of the American Church (more than half of the Catholics who had never set foot in Catholic schools still go to Mass every Sunday), it is still clear that the schools do indeed have an impact which by our sociological standards must be rated as substantial.

It should be noted, however, that Catholic education does not have identical impact on all children who attend it. We discovered in our research that the principal results of Catholic education were to be observed in those Catholics whose parents were reasonably devout and fervent Catholics to begin with. As a matter of fact, the most notable effects of Catholic education occurred only among those who had at least one parent who was a weekly communicant. This does not mean that the Catholic schools merely duplicate the efforts of the family. On the contrary, Catholics from good Catholic families who attended Catholic schools are much more different from Catholics from good families who did not attend Catholic schools, than are young people from poor Catholic families who attended Catholic schools different from those from poor Catholic families who did not attend Catholic schools. Far from replacing the work of the school, it would appear that the home reinforces what the school does, while the school in turn reinforces what the home does. Both are required to produce notable educational effects on the students.

The effects of attending Catholic school are also cumulative. No particular level—primary, secondary or higher—is more effective than any other level. It is only when the levels are combined that a truly impressive effect of religious education seemed to be observed. Thus, those who have attended Catholic colleges after having attended Catholic grammar school and high school

TABLE 2

COMPARISON OF OPINIONS OF THOSE WHO ATTENDED CATHOLIC COLLEGES WITH THOSE WHO ATTENDED OTHER COLLEGES

Questionnaire Item (Response in Parentheses)	Catholics		Q^a	Protestants (Percent)
	Catholic College (Percent)	Other College (Percent)		
Two people who are in love do not do anything wrong when they marry, even though one of them is divorced (agree)	24	50[b]	−.52	87[c]
White people have a right to live in an all-white neighborhood, and Negroes should respect this right (disagree strongly)	40	30	−.22	31
I would strongly disapprove if a Negro family moved next door to me (disagree strongly)	36	24[b]	−.28	27
Jews have too much power in the United States (disagree strongly)	75	57[b]	−.43	54[b]
People who don't believe in God have as much right to freedom of speech as anyone else (agree)	74	63	+.25	—
The Catholic Church teaches that large families are more Christian than small families (agree)	12	27[b]	−.46	—
The Protestant ministers should not be permitted to teach things publicly which are opposed to Catholic doctrine (disagree strongly)	67	44[b]	−.44	—
The Catholic Church teaches that a good Christian ought to think about the next life and not worry about fighting against poverty and injustice in this life (agree)	10	31[b]	−.60	—
Husband and wife may have sexual intercourse for pleasure alone (agree)	47	37	+.20	—
N	117	250	296	159

[a] Yule's Q is a form of the gamma association that is applied to two dichotomous variables.

[b] Significantly different from those who went to Catholic colleges.

[c] Significantly different from both Catholic groups.

are considerably different from those attending Catholic grammar school and high school and non-Catholic college, even when family religious background is held constant. As a matter of fact, at the college level an impact is had even on the social attitudes of Catholics. As Table 2 shows, Catholics who have attended Catholic colleges are far more enlightened in matters of race and anti-Semitism than college-educated Catholics who did not attend Catholic colleges. It would appear that religious education at the college or university level is rather effective in diminishing the amount of prejudice *if the way has been prepared by grammar school and high school.*

In addition to having its most notable effects on those who are predisposed for it by family background, or who have all their education in Catholic schools, Catholic education is also apparently considerably more successful among some ethnic groups than others, with the Irish and the Germans most disposed and Polish and Italian groups considerably less disposed to being influenced in their adult religious behavior by attending Catholic schools.

If, then, Catholic education in the United States is moderately successful religiously (and very considerably successful among certain ethnic, educational and religious groups), it must then be asked what price is paid by American Catholicism in isolating itself from the rest of society to achieve these effects. It has generally been assumed by critics of Catholic education, both inside and outside the Church, that the Catholic schools are divisive in that they tend to isolate Catholics from other Americans of different religious backgrounds. The argument is that if people do not attend school with members of other groups, they will not come to know the members of these groups and will have prejudice or unfavorable attitudes about them. This notion was put to a rigorous test in the NORC study and no substantiating evidence of any kind could be found. While those who attended Catholic schools were more likely to have Catholic friends while they were in school, there was no difference in having Catholic friends in adult life, nor in the choice of visitors to their homes, co-workers, marriage partners or neighbors. Furthermore, those who attended Catholic schools were just as likely to be involved in civic activities and in belonging to organizations that were not specifically Catholic. Finally, they were, if anything, somewhat more successful economically and academically than those Catholics who did not go to Catholic schools, even with family and social class held constant. Catholic school Catholics were more likely to go on to higher education and to have a higher prestige job and to make more money than public school Catholics, even when both groups started from roughly the same economic beginning.

In some instances these differences were quite striking. Thus, a Catholic who had attended a Catholic school and whose father had gone only to high school was himself more likely to go to college than a Catholic who attended public schools and whose father had gone to college. In other words, attendance at Catholic schools seemed to have compensated for the father's non-attendance of college in determining the educational achievement of the son.

Two other points should be noted before we turn to a discussion of the future of American Catholic education. First of all, it is important to determine and understand the difference between the short-run and long-run effect of Catholic education. Those adolescents studied in the NORC survey who were in Catholic schools were substantially different from adolescents in public schools. But the differences among adults, while they persisted, were not nearly so impressive, even among the adults in their twenties who had only recently departed from Catholic education. Apparently the schools have a powerful short-run effect, but if this is not reinforced either by a strong Catholic family life or marriage to a devout Catholic, the effect is rather quickly dissipated. Secondly, at least at the present time on the national average, the Confraternity of Christian Doctrine does not seem to be a particularly effective alternative for formal Catholic education. Those adolescents currently in CCD programs were very dissimilar in their attitudes and behavior from

Catholics in Catholic high schools and quite similar to the Catholics in public schools without any CCD experience. This finding remained true even when family religious background was held constant. Indeed, the authors of the NORC report were forced to conclude that on the national average at the present time CCD seems to be having very, very little impact. This is not to say that functional alternatives to a separate Catholic educational system cannot be found or that CCD cannot do a much more impressive job than it is doing. But in fact, these alternatives do not exist and CCD is quite unproductive at the present time.

Rather little could be found in either the NORC or the Notre Dame studies which would indicate serious questions about the survival of Catholic education in the United States in the foreseeable future. Far from diminishing the attractiveness of Catholic education, the improved social and economic condition of American Catholics seems to have led to a substantial growth in Catholic schooling. (In 1940, only 7 percent of the children in the country were in Catholic schools, while a quarter of a century later twice that proportion of American children were enrolled in Catholic primary or secondary institutions.) Secondly, while there are an increasing amount of parental complaints about Catholic schooling, it would appear from the NORC study that at the present time, at least, there is no necessary correlation between criticisms of Catholic schools and non-attendance, and it would further appear from the Notre Dame study that parental expectations of Catholic education are reasonably well satisfied. Finally, even though Catholic education is expensive and getting more expensive, the remarkable upward mobility of the Catholic population during the last quarter of a century of affluence has probably created a situation where a relatively smaller proportion of the income of the typical Catholic family needs to be devoted to religious education than was required twenty or thirty years ago. *If there is the desire to have a separate Catholic school system,* there is no reason to think the American Catholics do not have the financial resources to fulfill this desire. At the present time there seems to be no indication that the desire is waning, though given the rapid change that is going on in the whole Catholic Church, it might be unwise to predict developments too far into the future.

There can be no doubt, of course, that the Catholic schools in the United States have some fairly serious problems. The struggle for academic improvement (Catholic schools are probably on the average as good as most American schools but, all things considered, ought to be better) and for better religious training is moving ahead with at least some speed. More serious, however, for the long-run teaching of Catholic education is the opposition which exists to separate schools both among Catholics and among non-Catholics in the American population. The vast majority of American Catholic intellectuals, especially the most influential writers, have set their faces adamantly against Catholic education and do not hesitate to blame all the problems in the American Church on Catholic schools. There is something of a blind irrationality about much of this criticism which simply refuses to consider the possibility that empirical evidence might disprove some of the charges leveled against Catholic schools. Catholic education provides an excellent scapegoat for many Catholic intellectuals to release their frustrations and aggressions toward the institutional Church (frustrations and aggressions which at least in some instances are not by any means unjustified).

Further, even though non-Catholic opinions toward Catholic schools are rapidly becoming more favorable, there is still a hard core of academic and journalistic suspicion and opposition toward the schools. Even the staid and sober *New York Times*, which on most subjects makes every effort to be objective and fair, can readily become quite irrational when the subject of Catholic schools is raised. Nativism and anti-Catholicism are fast vanishing in American society. But for some reason as yet undiscovered, whatever traces of these phenomena remain can be stirred up by the thought of Catholic education.

Finally, the morale of many Catholic educators, especially the younger ones, is in some instances close to collapse. The steady criticism of the Catholic intellegentsia and the unfriend-liness of those outside the Church have caused many Catholic educators to wonder whether the system is worth the time, money and personnel that are poured into it and to question whether teaching in such a school is compatible with a religious or a priestly vocation. While Catholic schools are doing well finan-cially and improving academically, the ideological thrust within the system is not nearly as strong as it used to be, and the pride of the Catholics in their schools (or at least the pride of Catholic educators in their schools) again does not have nearly the power that it did in former years. It would seem, therefore, that for the long-run future of Catholic education in America, two things are necessary: (1) an elaborate public relations program that will counteract the unfavorable images the schools still have; (2) a renewed ideological thrust which will restore the confidence of Catholic educators. It must be confessed in all honesty that only minor progress has been made to date in both of these areas.

Two further developments seem to be in order. First of all, Catholic education must be assumed to include not only the formal Catholic schools but also the various classes for Catholics not in Catholic schools, adult education programs, marriage education and Newman work on the non-Catholic university campus. The schools probably will be most effective when they can be seen as a part of a much broader and more generalized approach to religious education. Secondly, lay people must re-ceive increasing responsibility and authority within Catholic edu-cation. While there is no great demand on the part of most lay people for such participation (only 1 percent of the NORC sam-ple mention this as something highly desirable), it is nevertheless quite necessary for the health and vitality of Catholic schools. In both of these areas, at least, promising beginnings have been made.

In summary, on the basis of the data available from recent studies, the separate Catholic school system in the United States, while not absolutely essential for the survival of the faith of the immigrants in the New World, has nonetheless made a fairly important contribution to the health and vitality of the American Church without producing any observable effects of isolating the Catholics from other Americans (at least beyond those isolating effects that religion itself has). The schools are particularly effective on certain ethnic groups, on people who attend them from grammar school to college, and on those who come prepared for the school by fervent religious backgrounds. The Catholic schools seem to be about as good academically as most American schools, and those who attended them are slightly more successful occupationally and academically than those who did not. While the short-run future looks reasonably bright, the opposition of journalists and intellectuals both inside and outside the Church could portend serious problems for Catholic education in the long run. Finally, much more research is needed in Catholic education both in America and in other countries so that, on the basis of data from several different cultures, broader generalizations can be made about the effectiveness of formal religious education in a classroom environment.

BIOGRAPHICAL NOTES

JAMES MCCLENDON: A Baptist, he was born March 6, 1924, in Louisiana, U.S.A. He studied at the University of Texas, at the Southwestern Baptist Seminary and at the Princeton Theological Seminary. He gained his doctorate in theology in 1952. At present he is associate professor of Protestant theology at the University of San Francisco. He is the author of *Pacemakers of Christian Thought* (1962).

MICHAEL HURLEY, S.J.: Born May 10, 1923, in Ireland, he joined the Jesuits and was ordained in 1954. He studied at the Jesuit Faculty of Philosophy (Tullamore, Ireland), in Louvain and at the Gregorian, gaining his doctorate in theology in 1960. At present he is teaching dogmatic theology at Milltown Park (Ireland). He is the author of *Church and Eucharist* (1966) and contributes to various journals, including *The Heythrop Journal* and *Irish Theological Quarterly*.

MAX THURIAN: A member of the Reformed Church, he was born August 16, 1921, in Geneva. He studied in the Faculty of Protestant Theology of the University of Geneva. He belongs to the Taizé Community where he is assistant to the Prior. His books include *Amour et Verité se recontrent* (1964), and he writes for *Verbum Caro*.

WALTER KASPER: Born March 5, 1933, in Germany, he was ordained in 1957. He studied at the Universities of Tübingen and Munich, gaining his doctorate in theology in 1961. Professor of dogmatic theology at the University of Münster, he is the author of several books and also writes for *Theologische Quartalschrift*.

DAVID STANLEY, S.J.: Born October 17, 1914, he joined the Jesuits and was ordained in 1946. He studied at St. Louis University and at the Pontifical Biblical Institute, Rome, gaining his doctorate in sacred scripture in 1952. He is professor of New Testament exegesis at Regis College, Willowdale (Canada) and associate professor of biblical theology at the State University of Iowa. He is the author of various books, including *The Apostolic Church in the New Testament*, and he writes for *Catholic Biblical Quarterly*.

JOHN MEYENDORFF: A member of the Orthodox Church, he was born February 17, 1926, in France. He studied at the Sorbonne and at the Institute of Orthodox Theology, Paris. He is professor of church history and of patristics at St. Vladimir's Orthodox Theological Seminary, New York. He is the author of *The Orthodox Church* (London, 1965) and other books, and is the editor of *St. Vladimir's Seminary Quarterly*.

RENZO BERTALOT: Born June 21, 1929, in Italy, he was ordained a minister of the Waldensian Church in 1954. He studied at the Theological Seminary, Princeton, and at McGill University, Montreal, gaining his master's degree in theology (1959) and his doctorate in philosophy (1962). He is the author of various books and writes for *Protestantismo* (Rome).

JOSEPH RATZINGER: Born in Germany, April 16, 1927, he was ordained in 1951. He studied at the Freissing College of Theology and at Munich University, gaining his doctorate in theology in 1953. He is professor of dogmatic theology and of the history of dogma at Tübingen University. He is co-author with Karl Rahner of *Revelation and Tradition* (London and New York, 1965) and author on his own account of numerous other books. He writes for *Catholica, Trierer theol. Zeitschrift* and other journals.

PIET SCHOONENBERG, S.J.: Born October 1, 1911, in Amsterdam, he joined the Jesuits and was ordained in 1939. He studied in the Theological Faculty, Maestricht, and at the Biblical Institute, Rome, gaining his doctorate in theology in 1948. He is now professor of dogmatic theology in the University of Nijmegen. He is the author of several books, including *Man and Sin* (1965), and contributes mainly to *Tijdschrift voor Theologie*.

WIM LUURT BOELENS, S.J.: Born April 23, 1925, in Holland, he joined the Jesuits and was ordained in 1958. He studied at Maestricht, Nijmegen and at Würzburg, gaining his doctorate in theology in 1963. He is responsible within his diocese for the encouragement of ecumenical activities. He is the author of several books and writes for *Oecumene*.

OLIVIER ROUSSEAU, O.S.B.: Born in Belgium, February 11, 1898, he was ordained in 1922. He studied at the Anselmo. He is editor of *Irénikon* and the author of various books, including *Monarchisme et vie religieuse* (1957) and *L'Orthodoxie et le mouvement oecuménique de 1920 à 1940* (*Ephem. theol. Lovan* 4, 1966).

JOHN M. OESTERREICHER: Born February 2, 1904, in Austria, he was ordained in 1927. He studied at the Universities of Vienna and Graz. He lectures in theology and is also director of the Institute of Judeo-Christian Studies, Newark, N.J. His publications include *The Israel of God* (1963); he is also editor of *The Bridge*.

ANDREW GREELEY: Born February 5, 1928, in America, he was ordained in 1954. He studied at the University of Chicago and gained his doctorate in philosophy in 1962, where he is now a lecturer in the Department of Sociology and Director of Studies, National Opinion Research Center. His publications include *The Education of Catholic Americans* (1966), written in collaboration with Peter H. Rossi, and he is associate editor of *The Review of Religious Research*.

International Publishers of CONCILIUM

ENGLISH EDITION
Paulist Press
Glen Rock, N. J., U.S.A.

Burns & Oates Ltd.
25 Ashley Place
London, S.W.1

DUTCH EDITION
Uitgeverij Paul Brand, N. V.
Hilversum, Netherlands

FRENCH EDITION
Maison Mame
Tours/Paris, France

GERMAN EDITION
Verlagsanstalt Benziger & Co., A.G.
Einsiedeln, Switzerland

Matthias Grunewald-Verlag
Mainz, W. Germany

SPANISH EDITION
Ediciones Guadarrama
Madrid, Spain

PORTUGUESE EDITION
Livraria Morais Editora, Ltda.
Lisbon, Portugal

ITALIAN EDITION
Editrice Queriniana
Brescia, Italy